CHAMPIONS OF FREEDOM

The Ludwig von Mises Lecture Series

CHAMPIONS OF FREEDOM
Volume 34

Great Economists
of the
Twentieth Century

Hillsdale College Press
Hillsdale, Michigan 49242

Hillsdale College Press

CHAMPIONS OF FREEDOM
The Ludwig von Mises Lecture Series—Volume 34
Great Economists of the Twentieth Century

©2006 Hillsdale College Press, Hillsdale, Michigan 49242

First printing 2006

The views expressed in this volume are not necessarily the views of Hillsdale College.

Printed in the United States of America

Front cover: (from left to right for each row)
Friedrich A. Hayek, photo © The Nobel Foundation
Ludwig von Mises, photo courtesy of Hillsdale College
John Maynard Keynes, photo © Corbis
Frank Knight, photo courtesy of Special Collections Research Center,
        University of Chicago Library
James Buchanan, photo © The Nobel Foundation
Milton Friedman, photo courtesy Milton Friedman

Library of Congress Control Number: 2006936138
ISBN-10: 0-91308-03-0
ISBN-13: 978-0-916308-03-2

Contents

Recommended Readings

Contributors

Robert J. Barro is Paul M. Warburg Professor of Economics at Harvard University, a senior fellow of the Hoover Institution of Stanford University, and a research associate of the National Bureau of Economic Research. Dr. Barro was recently president of the Western Economic Association and vice president of the American Economic Association. Co-editor of Harvard's *Quarterly Journal of Economics*, he writes occasionally for *The Wall Street Journal*, where he was previously a contributing editor. His current research concerns the impact of rare disasters on asset markets and the interplay between religion and political economy. His recent books include *Economic Growth, Nothing Is Sacred: Economic Ideas for the New Millennium,* and *Getting It Right: Markets and Choices in a Free Society.* He is currently completing a new intermediate macroeconomics text titled *Macroeconomics: A Modern Approach.*

Bruce Caldwell is the Joe Rosenthal Excellence Professor of Economics at the University of North Carolina at Greensboro. He is a past president of the History of Economics Society, a past Executive Director of the International Network for Economic Method, and a Life Member of Clare Hall, Cambridge. Dr. Caldwell serves on the editorial boards of seven academic journals and has held fellowships at New York University, Cambridge University, and the London School of Economics. His current research has focused on the writings of the Nobel Prize-winning economist and social theorist Friedrich A. Hayek. He is author of *Beyond Positivism: Economic Methodology in the 20th*

Century and an intellectual biography of Hayek titled *Hayek's Challenge.* Since 2002 Dr. Caldwell has been the General Editor of *The Collected Works of F. A. Hayek,* which will be the definitive scholarly collection of Hayek's writings.

Lee A. Coppock is an economics professor in the Department of Economics at the University of Virginia. Dr. Coppock has also taught economics and quantitative business courses for several years at Hillsdale College. He received his Ph.D. from George Mason University, where he had the privilege of studying under James Buchanan, the 1986 winner of the Nobel Prize in Economics. Dr. Coppock's current research is on economic growth rates across U.S. states. He has published articles in several journals, including *Economics Letters, The Southern Economic Journal,* and *Constitutional Political Economy.*

Donald J. Devine is the Grewcock Professor of American Values at Bellevue University, as well as a columnist, writer, adjunct scholar at the Heritage Foundation, and a political and management consultant. Dr. Devine is also the editor of ConservativeBattleline.com, the on-line publication of the American Conservative Union Foundation. He served as director of the U.S. Office of Personnel Management under President Reagan, as Reagan's deputy director of political planning, and as a regional director in his campaigns. He was senior political consultant for Bob Dole's and Steve Forbes' presidential campaigns, and has been a consultant to Republican committees and many GOP campaigns. For fourteen years, he was associate professor of government and politics at the University of Maryland, specializing in democratic theory and public opinion. Dr. Devine is the author of seven books, including, most recently, *In Defense of the West: American Values Under Siege.*

Richard M. Ebeling is president of the Foundation for Economic Education. Dr. Ebeling was formerly the Ludwig von Mises Professor of Economics and Chairman of the Department of Economics and Business Administration at Hillsdale College, and has also served as a vice president of the Future of Freedom Foundation. He is the editor of the three-volume work, *Selected Writings of Ludwig von Mises*—two volumes of which have been published by Liberty Fund Press—which is primarily based upon papers of Mises unearthed in a formerly secret Moscow archive. He edited several volumes in the *Champions of Freedom* series from Hillsdale College Press, as well as other works, including *The Dangers of Socialized Medicine* and *The Tyranny of Gun Control*. His most recent book is *Austrian Economics and the Political Economy of Freedom*. Dr. Ebeling is currently working on an intellectual biography of Ludwig von Mises.

Steve Forbes is president and CEO of Forbes and editor-in-chief of *Forbes* magazine. Since he assumed his position in 1990, the company has expanded to include *Forbes Asia*, *ForbesLife*, Forbes.com, Forbes Conference Group, and Forbes Custom Media. Mr. Forbes was born in Morristown, New Jersey, and he received a BA in history from Princeton University. At Princeton, he was the founding editor of *Business Today*, which became the country's largest magazine published by students for students and which is still being published currently by Princeton undergraduates. The holder of more than twenty honorary degrees, Mr. Forbes serves on the boards of the Ronald Reagan Presidential Foundation, the Heritage Foundation and the Foundation for the Defense of Democracies. He is on the Board of Overseers of the Memorial Sloan-Kettering Cancer Center and on the Board of Visitors for the School of Public Policy of Pepperdine University. In both 1996 and 2000, Mr. Forbes campaigned for the Republican nomination for the presidency. He is the author most recently of *Flat Tax Revolution: Using a Postcard to Abolish the IRS*.

Lord Robert Skidelsky is Professor of Political Economy at Warwick University in England. Lord Skidelsky is a director of the Moscow School of Political Studies, founding member of the World Political Forum, and a member of the Advisory Council of the School of Advanced International and Area Studies, Shanghai University. He has written numerous articles on the economic and political aspects of international relations, including, most recently, "Keynes, Globalization and the Bretton Woods Institutions in the Light of Changing

Ideas about Markets." The author of *The World After Communism*, he is currently working on a book on globalization and international relations. His three-volume biography of the economist John Maynard Keynes received numerous prizes, including the Lionel Gelber Prize for International Relations and the Council on Foreign Relations Prize for International Relations. Lord Skidelsky was made a life peer in 1991 and elected a Fellow of the British Academy in 1994.

Mark Skousen, professional economist, investment expert, university professor, and author of over twenty books, holds the Benjamin Franklin Chair of Management at Grantham University. In 2004–2005, he taught economics and finance at Columbia Business School, Barnard College, and Columbia University. Since 1980, Skousen has been editor-in-chief of *Forecasts & Strategies*, an award-winning investment newsletter. He is also chairman of *Investment U*, one of the largest investment e-letters in the country. He is a former analyst for the CIA, a columnist to *Forbes* magazine, and past president of the Foundation for Economic Education (FEE). He has written for *The Wall Street Journal*, *Forbes*, and *Reason* magazine. His bestsellers include *The Making of Modern Economics*, *The Power of Economic Thinking*, *Vienna and Chicago*, and *Friends or Foes?* In 2006, he compiled and edited *The Compleated Autobiography, by Benjamin Franklin*. In honor of his work in economics, finance and management, Grantham University renamed its business school, "The Mark Skousen School of Business."

Foreword

For 34 years we have collected the papers delivered at our annual Ludwig von Mises Lecture Series at Hillsdale College into book form, calling the series "Champions of Freedom." This volume, consisting of papers delivered in February of this year, has as its theme the great economists of the twentieth century.

The last of the economists discussed herein is Milton Friedman, winner of the Nobel Prize for Economics in 1976 and recipient of the Presidential Medal of Freedom in 1988. Dr. Friedman pioneered the "Chicago School" of economics, wrote many seminal books, and served as an advisor to three presidents.

Milton has also been a longtime friend of Hillsdale College. Just this past May, he was the keynote speaker at our National Leadership Seminar in San Francisco, which commemorated the 25th anniversary of his and his wife Rose's book, *Free to Choose: A Personal Statement*.

Two weeks ago we were saddened to hear of Milton's death at the age of 94. He will be remembered as one of the most stalwart and influential defenders of individual liberty of our time.

We dedicate this volume of Champions of Freedom to his memory.

LARRY P. ARNN
President
Hillsdale College
November 30, 2006

Introduction

This volume of Champions of Freedom, the Ludwig von Mises Lecture Series, gives an insider's view of six of the great economists of the twentieth century. The authors who write about Milton Friedman and James Buchanan are not only scholars who have studied the work of these great economists, they know their subjects personally. The authors of the essays on John Maynard Keynes, Frank Knight, Ludwig von Mises, and Friedrich Hayek are renowned experts on the history of economic thought and the works of these economists. The editor of one of the world's premier business magazines discusses the battle between collectivism and free markets, a topic found in the writings of each of the great economists. An eminent political scientist provides insights on recent political trends and the relationship between the advances in economic theory these economists engendered and the translation of those ideas into public policy.

The six economists in this volume cover a range of thought. It includes, for example, John Maynard Keynes, as well as some of his fiercest critics. (Mises once wrote that "Keynes was not an innovator.... His contribution consisted rather in providing an apparent justification for the policies which were popular with those in power in spite of the fact that all economists viewed then as disastrous.")[1] The men discussed in this book include the teacher and mentor to several Nobel Prize winners, Austrian School economists, and the founder of Public Choice Theory. What is common to these six economists is what sets them apart from others: Not only are they all eminent scholars, their collective innovations have had a lasting influence on economic thought and public policy. All iconoclasts of a sort, none were afraid to go against the grain of accepted opinion.

Robert Skidelsky examines the interrelationship among the writings of Keynes, Friedman, and Hayek. While many would think that Keynes and Friedman were polar opposites in their views of the economic system, Skidelsky brings out the similarities in their analyses. The three economists might find common ground in their recognition of uncertainty and information deficiencies in the economy. Keynes was not simply an academic concerned with advancing his reputation among the intellectual elite; he had a passion for putting his theories into practice. His career was marked by extensive public service, both formal and informal. Skidelsky provides insights into Keynes's early training and how he changed the way economists analyze the overall economic system. He relates how Keynes's early work on probability theory is related to his theory of business cycles. Especially interesting is Skidelsy's analysis of the ways Keynes's formulations differed from the existing paradigm, how Keynes rearranged the framework of the business cycle debate, and the extent to which Keynes influenced public policy both during his lifetime and after.

Mark Skousen's essay is an excellent observation of Frank Knight as scholar, teacher, and individual. Knight's many writings provoke thought rather than present a body of consistent thought laid out through a model of economic order. Skousen highlights the side of Knight that would have displeased Harry Truman, who once asked for a one-handed economist because economists always say "on the one hand this, and on the other hand that." Knight's legacy lies in his challenge to readers and students to take his insights as a basis from which to begin to think for themselves. Perhaps this is why he counted three Nobel Laureates among his students.

Richard Ebeling's discussion of Ludwig von Mises benefits both from his personal relationship with Mrs. Mises and from his years of scholarly attention to the writings of the Austrian school. Mises was one of the most prescient economists of the twentieth century. During the 1920s he gave a complete argument for the failure of socialism, logically showing that it cannot provide wealth for the many. In 1927, his small volume, *Liberalism*, countered academic and popular opinion, and essentially predicted the economic collapse brought by the Great Depression, the failure of public works projects to reduce unemployment, and the advent of World War II. Mises demonstrated that capitalism is the only economic system that can create wealth for all, that it is consistent with individual liberty, and that it promotes world peace. Professor Ebeling has been instrumental in keeping Mises's writings alive and carrying on the exchange of ideas that Mises believed would lead to a better society.

Robert Barro's paper is an introduction not just to the works of Milton Friedman, but to the man as well. Professor Barro is able to draw on his long-time friendship with Friedman to give the reader a feeling for the inner workings of the great economist. While Friedman does not believe that an academic economist should attempt to influence policy by accepting a position in government, he is certainly very concerned with the implementation of his ideas. Friedman felt that an academic can best serve by making the case for certain policies by demonstrating the logical correctness of one's argument, testing it empirically, and then explaining it to the mass audience. His book *Free to Choose*, and the documentary based on it, fit within this strategy. In the end, Friedman has had an influence on a raft of issues, such as monetary rules, school choice, privatization of social security, and a flat rate income tax. In each case, Friedman, like the other economists discussed in this volume, stood by his ideas in the face of criticism from the mainstream of his profession and eventually turned his analysis into the accepted wisdom.

Bruce Caldwell, the eminent Hayekian scholar, examines who, among the great economists discussed in this volume, has the broadest scope. Friedrich Hayek's works were initially greeted by the profession as anachronistic and reactionary. Like Mises, he battled hard against the ideas of central planning and delved deeply into the problems of information that condemned central planning to failure. Winning the Nobel Prize almost brought him into mainstream recognition, but even today the wealth of knowledge presented in Hayek's extensive writings is not given sufficient recognition. Reading just the endnotes to his *Constitution of Liberty* provides the reader with a gold mine of information and research.

Lee A. Coppock was a student of James Buchanan at George Mason University, in Fairfax, Virginia, where Professor Buchanan still resides. Coppock's essay covers not only Buchanan's work on Public Choice, for which he is most renowned, but provides enlightenment of a broad range of his important work. Once again we have an economist who challenges the mainstream thought, suffering isolation until his ideas eventually became accepted. Coppock points out that Buchanan, a student of Frank Knight, was somewhat conflicted in his early years at Chicago, describing himself as a Libertarian-Socialist. Buchanan's early work on externalities and clubs undermined the case for government as necessarily superior to markets in the case of externalities and public goods. His *Calculus of Consent* took the issue one step further and addressed government failure as the counterpoint to the work on market failure being done at the time. Buchanan showed that while one may not like the market outcome, one cannot assume a benevolent government that will improve the outcome. One must instead understand how government works, and understand the system incentives that individuals acting as politicians and bureaucrats follow, in order to determine the best policy.

Sherlock Holmes once chastised Dr. Watson by saying, "you see but you do not observe." Steve Forbes is an observer. His essay discusses how the West drifted into acceptance of central planning and the unobserved aspects of market capitalism. In particular, Forbes delves into the morality of capitalism, and presents his argument for how capitalism can gain the moral high ground. As he points out, "philanthropy and business, charity and democratic capitalism are not opposites, but two sides of the same coin." He updates Mises's point that the only way to succeed in a capitalist society is to please others. Rather than decry the advances of capitalism as mainstream media has a tendency to do, Forbes shows how the market process benefits the poor, the environment, and the moral standing of society.

Political scientist Donald Devine examines how the politics of the twentieth century have responded to the great economic debate over socialism and capitalism. Devine questions why the superiority of markets over socialism has been established in the economic community, even as we witness the ever-present growth of government. This is particularly disconcerting when both houses of Congress—as well as the presidency—are under the control of the political party most associated with limited government. Devine believes that because politicians are able to manipulate public opinion, they take advantage of a rationally ignorant public to expand their power base, which is government. As he puts it: Politics trumps economics.

This volume, as well as the conference from which these essays came, lays testimony to the triumph of intellectuals who are willing to overturn the existing paradigm, even if it means being an outcast for much of their careers. While Keynes's ideas were used to expand the role of government, even he thought his theories were a counterpoint to socialism. The rest of the six great economists honored here are staunch defenders of individual liberty and market capitalism as the social order. While Steve Forbes demonstrates that a major media outlet is capable of making a clear and reasoned case for limited government and reliance on markets, Devine believes that the case for liberty needs to be carried forward into the political realm. Readers of this volume will be well-prepared for the task.

GARY WOLFRAM
George Munson Professor
of Political Economy
Hillsdale College

Note

[1]Ludwig von Mises, *Planning for Freedom*, 4th ed. (Spring Mills, PA: Libertarian Press, 1980), p. 69.

STEVE FORBES

The Great (and Continuing) Economic Debate of the Twentieth Century

The great economic debate of the twentieth century was between collectivists and free marketers. In one sense, the free marketers won: When the Berlin Wall fell in 1989, it was widely acknowledged that Soviet socialism had been a catastrophic, not to say murderous, failure. But in another sense, the debate continues. Democratic capitalism still has not vanquished the idea of collectivism. Far from it.

At the beginning of the last century, free markets seemed to be on the ascendancy everywhere. But two events gave collectivism its lease on life. The first was World War I. In addition to the slaughter—and to breeding the ideologies of communism, state fascism, Nazism, and even the Islamic extremism we are battling today—World War I served as an intoxicating drug to those in the West who believed that a handful of people in government could manage affairs better than the messy way in which free peoples tend to do so. Massive increases in government powers, coupled with massive increases in taxation, gave many the idea that we can achieve massive increases in production by commandeering the financial resources of society.

The second event that served as a boon to collectivism was the Great Depression, which was widely seen as a free market failure. This view was false. Misguided government policies were at fault— the Smoot-Hawley Tariff, for instance, which dried up the flow of capital into and out of the country. If you track the stock market crash of 1929, it parallels the course of this tariff bill through Congress. When Smoot-Hawley arose in the fall of 1929, the markets fell; when it looked like the tariff bill was sidetracked in late 1929, the markets revived (the Dow Jones went up 50 percent from its lows in November); in the spring of 1930 it was signed into law, and the rest is history.

There were other factors at work in the Great Depression, of course, such as President Hoover's gigantic tax increases of 1931. But despite the fact that these also involved bad policies, the lesson taken away by many was that economies will implode unless the government manages them. John Maynard Keynes, the intellectual guiding light behind New Deal economics, believed that an economy was like a machine: If you put doses of money into or pull money out at the right times, he thought you could achieve an equilibrium. This idea that government can drive an economy as if it were an automobile has had baleful consequences.

Other leading economists at the time, such as Joseph Schumpeter, recognized that an economy is an aggregate of disparate activities—thus, the idea of achieving equilibrium, while it makes for a neat theory, is nonsense in the real world. A vibrant economy is full of constant disequilibria: New enterprises rise up, old ones decline, and so on. Snapshots of such economies mean very little. In the real world, therefore, free markets operate rationally and efficiently in a way that government regulators simply cannot.

Here in America we came to this realization at the end of the 1970s. Following World War II, we largely bought into the idea that government must play an active role to prevent the economy from going off the cliff. But in the late 1970s, the devastation of inflation and high taxes brought about a reassessment. With the election of Ronald Reagan, the U.S. took a step back from Keynesian economics. Since then, as Western Europe has stagnated—creating, for instance, only a fraction of the private-sector jobs that the U.S. has created—our country has undergone an economic revival.

Nonetheless, democratic capitalism often still seems to be on the defensive. Why?

Is Democratic Capitalism Good?

One of the great vulnerabilities of capitalism is the perception that it is somehow less than moral, if not positively amoral. A common view of business was depicted in the movie *Wall Street*, in which Michael Douglas's character made famous the phrase, "Greed is good." Capitalism is widely seen as promoting selfishness. We tolerate it because it gives us jobs and prosperity, but many look on this as a Faustian bargain. Charity and capitalism are seen as polar opposites. Thus there is a phrase that is often used today—I myself use it from time to time without thinking—which is "giving back." If you have succeeded in business, it is counted a good thing if you "give back" to the community. Charity is, of course, a good thing. The problem with this phrase is its implication that by succeeding we have taken something that wasn't ours. The same idea is summed up in the cynical saying, "Behind every great fortune lies a great crime." This way of thinking about democratic capitalism is wrong.

In fact, philanthropy and capitalism are two sides of the same coin. To succeed in business in a free market economy, one must meet the needs and wants of others. Someone may have a terrible personality—and be the kind of person who makes babies cry, or who thinks that he or she is only in business to make money for himself/herself—but the bottom line is that such individuals can only succeed if they produce a product or service that people want. This system weaves intricate webs of cooperation that we don't even think about. Someone who opens a restaurant assumes that farmers will grow the food, that processors will process and package it, and that truckers will deliver it (once they have been supplied the fuel to do so by the oil companies, and on and on). These marvelous webs of cooperation happen every day throughout a free economy. No one is commanding it. It occurs spontaneously in a way that economists like Schumpeter understood.

Free markets force people to look to the future and take risks. Misers do not found companies like Microsoft. Nor should we look on it as immoral for people to work for the betterment of themselves and their families. We are all born with God-given talents, and it is right to develop them to the fullest. The great virtue of democratic capitalism is that it guarantees that as we develop our talents, we are contributing to the public good. Statistics show that the United States is both the most commercial nation and the most philanthropic nation in human history. This is no paradox. The two go hand-in-hand.

Another vulnerability of democratic capitalism is that although it leads to progress and to an increase in our societal standard of living, progress is usually disruptive. This allows collectivists to play on people's natural fear of change. We saw this with the rise of industrialism in the nineteenth century. The paintings and writings of that time often depicted a pastoral agricultural past. Then railroads came along to disrupt the canals, and cars came along to disrupt the railroads. Buggy-whip makers and blacksmiths were done for. One can imagine what *60 Minutes* would have been investigating 100 years ago: poor blacksmiths being put out of work by Henry Ford. Likewise, when TV came along in the late 1940s and early 1950s, most movie theaters in the country went broke. Now the Internet is disrupting newspapers and Craig's List is disrupting classified advertising. Disruptions are inevitable in a free market system. The political challenge is to allow these disruptions to take place—they are ultimately constructive, after all—rather than reacting in a way that stymies progress.

In recent decades, collectivists have hijacked the cause of environmentalism to promote their agenda. I am not talking about the desire to have clean water or clean air; we are all in favor of that. One of the great accomplishments of the last century was removing lead from the air we breathe. Saving tigers and elephants from extinction is also a good thing. I am talking about using the mantra of environmentalism to try to control the economy in the way the old-time socialists wanted to, by breathing hellfire and damnation on those who don't subscribe to that new religion. But if the goal is to improve the environment, increasing government regulation and destroying manufacturing is counterproductive. Affluence is the friend, not the enemy, of the environment. As people become better off, they want a higher quality of living, including environmental improvements. And it is new technology that drives such improvements. Consider the East coast of the United States. Even though its population has more than doubled—in some areas, it has tripled—and even though there are more developments, malls, and urban sprawl, there are more trees on the East coast today than there were 80 years ago. Why? Technology allows us to grow more food on less land. Technology is a friend of the environment.

Additional Collectivist Myths

Three additional myths are used to promote collectivism. One is the idea that demand is the key to economic growth. Collectivist economists often talk about means to increase "aggregate demand," as if that would ensure that the economy will grow. Following Keynes, they assume that the economy is like a machine. But again, the economy is an aggregate of tens of millions of people, millions of businesses, millions of technologies. We don't know how it interacts on a day-to-day basis. We don't know what's going to work or not work. Who could have conceived of eBay 10 to 12 years ago? Today, 400,000 people make their livings on eBay. When Google was launched, there were ten other search engines. Who would have thought another one was needed? But Google found a way to do it better and ended up on top.

Innovation is the key. No matter what the industry—railroads, cars, computers, or the Internet—risk-taking is messy. It is often irrational, and seemingly wasteful. But it is the only way to determine what works and what doesn't.

Another collectivist myth concerns trade. If I were dictator of the world, even though I believe in the First Amendment, I would ban trade numbers, especially merchandise trade numbers. They just lead to mischief. We are given the impression that a trade surplus is like a profit and a trade deficit is like a loss. But trade is not a transaction between countries. It takes place between parties. For example, *Forbes* magazine buys paper. For the 88 years we have been in existence, we have run a trade deficit with our paper suppliers. If you look at just that trade deficit, you might think we are doing poorly. But if you look at the two parties involved, you see that this is not the case. The paper supplier thinks he's going to make money selling his paper. We think we're going to make money by taking the paper and putting print on it, adding value. So it is a mutually profitable transaction, even if it looks like a trade deficit. Or consider the act of having a book printed in Taiwan. Looking at the trade number alone, it appears there is a $2 trade deficit with Taiwan. Yet when the printed book arrives in the U.S., it retails for $24.95. The value is added here. The author gets a cut, the publisher gets a cut, the booksellers get a cut, the distributors get a cut, and the remainder stores get a cut. Something similar happened with the iPod: A lot of its parts are made overseas, but where is most of the value added? Here in the United States. North America has had a merchandise trade deficit for 350 out of the last 400 years, and we have done very well, thank you.

The final myth concerns budget deficits. Milton Friedman said several years ago that if he had a choice between a federal budget of $1 trillion that was in the red and a federal budget of $2 trillion that was balanced, he would take the former. Deficits, in and of themselves, are not evil. Deficits must be put in context, because Washington's inability to curb spending is often used as an excuse to raise taxes.

Principles of Prosperity

There are five basic principles of economic growth.

First and foremost is the rule of law: Without individual equality before the law, entrepreneurs cannot challenge already existing businesses. Alliances between the latter and government regulators who place barriers before entrepreneurs must be guarded against.

The second essential principle is property rights. We take for granted in this country that if you buy a piece of property everyone acknowledges that you own it. Most countries don't have that kind of uniform property system. A few years ago, Hernando DeSoto, a great economist from Peru, saw that in countries like his, although there is entrepreneurial activity, there isn't the corresponding prosperity found in the U.S. And he wondered why. In his recent book, *The Mystery of*

Capital: Why Capitalism Triumphs in the West and Fails Everywhere Else,[1] one of the key factors he cites is the absence of a legal foundation for property rights in so many countries. In Brazil's shantytowns, an individual may know that he owns the house in which he lives, and his neighbors may know it, but the fact is not recognized elsewhere.

Mr. DeSoto was asked by the Egyptian government a few years ago to determine who owns the businesses and residences in Egypt. His finding was that 88 percent of the businesses in Egypt are illegal. Why is that? Here in the U.S., it is possible to set up a business legally in a matter of days. In Egypt, it takes a couple of years. It requires dealing with numerous bureaucracies—and doling out numerous bribes. It makes sense to proceed "informally." On the other hand, running a business outside the law limits its growth. Most "informal" enterprises never grow beyond the level of family enterprises, because if they get too big, they might attract the attention of the tax collector.

DeSoto's group also reported that 92 percent of Egyptian housing is illegal. A family may have a deed to their house, but only a few miles away, that deed won't be recognized. In Egypt, as in so many other places, there is no uniform system of establishing and protecting property rights. As a result, four billion people around the world own $9 trillion of assets that amount to dead capital.

What do I mean by "dead capital"? Remember that in the U.S., the most important source of capital for new ventures is not Wall Street, the local banker, or the venture capitalist. It is the mortgage market. To finance a business start-up, people often increase their mortgage or take out a second mortgage. This is not possible in countries like Egypt. Understanding this was key to Japan's post-World War II economic boom. General MacArthur reformed a feudalistic property system, from one in which the peasants had only an informal system of property exchange into a system with formalized property rights. Immediately, the Japanese economy took off. The importance of property rights is not sufficiently recognized by those of us who take them for granted.

The third principle of economic prosperity is low taxes. Taxes are not just a means of raising revenue for the government. They are also a price. Income taxes are a price paid for working; taxes on profits are the price paid for being successful in business; taxes on capital gains are the price paid for taking risks. In light of this, the importance of low taxes is easy to see: When the price of good things is low—like work, success, and risk-taking—you tend to get more of them. Raise the price of these good things and you get fewer of them. In 2003, tax rates were lowered in the U.S., and the economy started to grow again. As we have seen time and again, tax cuts do not mean a loss of tax revenue. By increasing incentives, the government comes out ahead. Washington's revenues in the last fiscal year were up 15 percent—$100 billion above expectations. Washington's problem is not revenue, but spending.

The fourth principle is making it simpler to launch legal businesses. Getting bureaucracy out of the way will inject a new vibrancy into an economy.

The fifth and final principle is free trade. Expanding markets and creating greater opportunity for trade benefits us all.

The great economic debate continues into the twenty-first century, despite the proven superiority of free markets in terms of delivering prosperity, because misperceptions are keeping democratic capitalism from capturing the moral high ground. Dispelling these misperceptions should be our priority as we carry on that debate in the years ahead.

Note

[1]Hernando DeSoto, *The Mystery of Capital: Why Capitalism Triumphs in the West and Fails Everywhere Else* (New York: Basic Books, 2003).

Bruce Caldwell

Friedrich A. Hayek: Economist, Social Theorist, and Philospher of Liberty

My interest in Friedrich A. Hayek, the polymath economist, social theorist, and philosopher of liberty, has turned into fascination.

I did not come to Hayek as a conservative or a libertarian; I came to him as an intellectual historian, a historian of economic thought. There are a number of obvious reasons why a historian of thought might find Hayek interesting.

1. He lived a long time. Born in 1899, he died in 1992: His life spanned the twentieth century.
2. He was a prolific writer. His first significant work was a student essay on psychology, completed in 1920, which became the starting point for his remarkable book on psychology, *The Sensory Order.* His last book, *The Fatal Conceit,* appeared in 1988.
3. His archives are massive. Housed at the Hoover Institution at Stanford, the Hayek archives keep growing; there are now 130 boxes. To give an idea of what this means, his extensive correspondence with Karl Popper fills only two folders in Box 44—and that box contains 29 other folders as well.
4. He was controversial. People either love or hate Hayek, which has given rise to multiple interpretations of his work. Some of these interpretations are very bad, and correcting bad interpretations is what historians of thought try to do.
5. He had a knack for being at the right place at the right time. This point requires some elaboration.

Hayek grew up in fin de siécle Vienna, one of the most fertile places and moments in the history of modern Western thought. He learned economics from Friedrich von Wieser and Ludwig von Mises: the former was his major professor, the latter became his mentor. Among his classmates were people like Oskar Morgenstern, one of the inventors of game theory. After university he went to the United States and, armed with letters of introduction from Joseph Schumpeter, he met the most prominent American economists. He sat in on the American institutionalist Wesley Clair Mitchell's history of economic thought class, and gave the last paper in J. B. Clark's last seminar.

In the early 1930s, Lionel Robbins invited Hayek to the London School of Economics. (As I tell my students, if you go to the main library at LSE today, you are in the Lionel Robbins building.) This led to his appointment, at the age of 32, to a named chair. Upon his arrival he engaged in a series of debates with some of the leading lights of the profession. He debated with John Maynard Keynes and Piero Sraffa over monetary theory and the theory of the business cycle; with Frank Knight and Nicholas Kaldor over capital theory; with Oskar Lange and Evan Durbin over socialism. On his friend Gottfried Haberler's recommendation, Hayek invited the Austrian philosopher Karl Popper to give a paper in his seminar, and was instrumental in bringing Popper to the London School of Economics after the war. In 1950 he moved to the Committee on Social Thought at the University of Chicago, just as the Chicago School of economics was being formed by Milton Friedman, Aaron Director, and, a little later, George Stigler—all of whom Hayek had invited to the first Mont Pèlerin meeting, which he organized in 1947.

Hayek knew all of the best minds of the profession. In telling Hayek's story, one also tells, from a specific point of view, the story of the development of economics in the twentieth century. I say from a specific point of view because Hayek disagreed with just about everyone he came into contact with. If he was always in the right place at the right time, it was usually with the wrong ideas—or so it must have seemed to his contemporaries.

Hayek first began his assault on socialism in the 1930s, when all right-minded people viewed it as a middle way between a failed capitalist system and the totalitarianisms of the fascist and communist variety.

He famously dubbed this mistake "the muddle of the middle." As an Austrian School economist he was suspicious of the use of aggregates in economics because they hide the relative price movements that are so fundamental to the workings of a market. Thus he was a critic of the Keynesian revolution before it had even properly taken place. He was greatly skeptical of the merits of empirical work (a position he shared with Keynes, as well as others), devoting the first chapter of his first book, *Monetary Theory and the Trade Cycle*, to its critique. Because of this, he missed the econometrics revolution. Though he helped introduce general equilibrium analysis to English-speaking economists, he also questioned its usefulness for shedding light on the workings of a dynamic market process: Thus he missed the formalist revolution of the 1950s as well. Just when specialization was sweeping the scientific disciplines, his work was increasingly multidisciplinary and integrative. When not dismissed as reactionary or anachronistic, as was the case with his economic and political philosophy, Hayek's work was ignored, as with the case of his book on psychology. In short, he was a man almost systematically out of step with his time.

Hayek's response to this was classic. He sat down and quietly tried to figure out why so many supposedly smart people got so many things wrong. His answer was very appealing to a historian of ideas: In such works as "Scientism and the Study of Society," "The Counter-Revolution of Science," and "Individualism: True and False," he identified a complex of ideas that had gradually but inexorably led the West to embrace what he called "the scientistic prejudice" or "the planning mentality," both variants of what he ultimately dubbed "constructivist rationalism."

This makes Hayek a fascinating figure. What is truly remarkable, though, is how often over the course of time the *ideas* of this academic gadfly have come to be vindicated.

Hayek is most famous for his critique of socialism, a project that built on the work of his mentor, Ludwig von Mises. Mises had noted that in its purest form socialism calls for the total abolition of private firms, which are replaced by state ownership of the means of production. But if the state owns the means of production, there are no markets in which factors of production are bought and sold. Consequently no prices are attached to them. Mises pointed out that the absence of market prices means that factory managers have no information about which resources are relatively scarce and which are relatively plentiful. He concluded that socialist economies would be much less efficient in using resources than free market economies. Market prices inform market participants about the relative scarcity of goods; by bidding for them, market participants help ensure that resources flow toward their highest valued uses.

Hayek's contributions nicely complement those made by von Mises. He focused on what would come to be called "the knowledge problem"; that is, how to coordinate human action in a world in which knowledge is dispersed. For Hayek, the market system was a key coordinating mechanism. In a market system, millions of agents make millions of consumption and production decisions every day. Their decisions are based in part on the vast array of prices that they confront in the market, prices that give them information about relative scarcities. But in addition, agents have access to particular bits of knowledge that are specific to time and place, some of them tacit. This knowledge shapes the decisions that are made. Because their market activity reflects this local knowledge, the actions these agents decide to make causes this information to become embedded in the array of market prices. In short, market activity is both *price-determined* (prices shape what people do) and *price-determining* (what people do, based on local knowledge, determines what prices are). In this way market prices coordinate the specific knowledge of time and place possessed by millions of market agents. Freely adjusting market prices act as a giant communication network.

Hayek began having these insights in the 1930s, but his clearest statement of them is, perhaps, in his seminal 1945 article, "The Use of Knowledge in Society," which is still quoted today by economists working in the economics of information.

In addition to articulating how markets work, Hayek's arguments undermined the various socialist proposals that were on offer, most of which required some form of price fixing. For those who replaced this with "trial and error" adjustment procedures, Hayek questioned whether such a process undertaken by a state bureaucracy could ever match the speed of adjustment provided by a dynamic market process, fueled as it is by the actions of alert entrepreneurs for whom every error represents a profit opportunity. Still other of his opponents made arguments that went far beyond economics. These socialists promised a society that was not only more efficient than capitalism, but also more just, where individuals have more self-determination and greater political freedom, and where scientific reasoning would be used to improve upon a host of outdated social institutions. To challenge these utopian visions, Hayek needed to develop political, historical, and ethical arguments against them. He did this in what was to become his most famous book, *The Road to Serfdom.*

Against the idea that democratic socialism would bring with it greater political freedom, Hayek countered that planning the economy would soon lead to increased political control. One virtue of a market economy is that it allows people to express their very different tastes and, for those with the means, to get them satisfied. In a planned economy, socialist managers must decide which goods, and how much of them, are produced. Any particular mix of goods will be favored by some groups and opposed by others. Gridlock will ensue. If progress is to be made, even democratically elected socialist regimes will at some point be forced to make decisions for the people, which is much easier to do if political dissension is suppressed. To run a fully planned economy successfully, Hayek claimed that its socialist managers ultimately must secure control of the political process as well. If one looks at the world and examines those economies where top-down central planning has been put into effect, it is clear that restrictions—often severe—on both political and personal freedoms either accompanied the move or followed very soon thereafter.

Though famous as a critic of socialism, Hayek made a number of positive contributions to social theory. In such books as *The Constitution of Liberty* and *Law, Legislation and Liberty,* he made the case for a return to a liberal constitutional democratic market order. I use all those adjectives to signal that Hayek was no Dr. Pangloss about laissez-faire: He believed that a market system by itself holds few guarantees. It is only when embedded in a set of other social institutions—a democratic polity, with strong constitutional protection of a private sphere of individual activity, operating under the rule of law, with laws that are general, prospective, and reasonably stable, with well-defined, enforced, and transferable property rights—would a market system have a chance of working. In these mature works Hayek expounds his philosophy of liberty, describing and defending the complex of institutions, norms, and beliefs that he felt would best promote the discovery, transmission, and use of knowledge so that individuals are able to use that knowledge to succeed in the pursuit of their chosen goals. Hayek's ideas have been taken as foundational by such later Nobel Prize winners as Douglass North and Vernon Smith, whose works in new institutional economics and experimental economics, respectively, seek in their own ways to find the appropriate institutional mix for a free society.

This only touches on some of Hayek's contributions. His work on the informational role of prices is, of course, now considered a seminal insight within economics. His work on complex self-generating and adaptive "spontaneous orders" has piqued the interest of those exploring the relevance of complexity theory, neural network models, and agent-based computational models for economic and social analysis. Philosophers of mind, evolutionary biologists, and neuroscientists have been attracted to his view of the brain as a hierarchical classifier system, as revealed in his remarkable book on the foundations of psychology, *The Sensory Order.*

Most remembered as a philosopher of liberty, F. A. Hayek was also a polymath social theorist. Fascinating in itself, his intellectual journey helps us to better comprehend the contours of the development of twentieth-century social thought. A man of ideas, his life demonstrates the vital importance of ideas in the ongoing battle for liberty.

.

RICHARD M. EBELING

Ludwig von Mises:
The Political Economist of Liberty

Over a professional career that spanned almost three-quarters of the twentieth century, the Austrian economist Ludwig von Mises was without any exaggeration one of the leading and most important defenders of economic liberty. The ideas of individual freedom, the market economy, and limited government that he defended in the face of the rising tide of socialism, fascism, and the interventionist welfare state have had few champions as clear and persuasive as Mises. It is also certainly the case that he was the most comprehensive and consistent critic of all forms of modern collectivism. Furthermore, his numerous writings on the political, economic, and social principles of classical liberalism and the market order remain as fresh and relevant as when he penned them decades ago.[1]

Born in the city of Lemberg in the old Austro-Hungarian Empire on September 29, 1881, Mises came from a prominent family of Jewish merchants and businessmen. A few months before Ludwig was born, his great-grandfather, Mayer Rachmiel Mises, was honored with a nobility title for his service to the Emperor Franz Joseph as a leader of the Jewish community in Lemberg.[2]

Ludwig's father, Arthur, moved his family to Vienna in the early 1890s where he worked as a civil engineer for the Imperial railway system. Ludwig attended one of the city's leading academic gymnasiums as preparation for university studies. He entered the University of Vienna in 1900, and received his doctoral degree in jurisprudence in 1906. In 1909, he was employed by the Vienna Chamber of Commerce, Crafts, and Industry, and continued to work at the Chamber as a senior economic analyst until he left Vienna in 1934 to accept a full-time teaching position at the Graduate Institute of International Studies in Geneva. In addition to his work at the Chamber, Mises taught at the University of Vienna, lead an internationally renowned interdisciplinary private seminar, and founded the Austrian Institute for Business Cycle Research in 1927, with a young Friedrich A. Hayek as its first director.[3]

It was during his years in Geneva, between 1934 and 1940, that Mises wrote his greatest work in economics, *Human Action: A Treatise on Economics*.[4] In the summer of 1940, as the Nazi war machine was finishing its conquest of Western Europe, Mises and his wife made their way from Switzerland to the United States, where he spent the rest of his life continuing his writings and teaching at New York University. He died October 10, 1973, at the age of 92.

In both Vienna between the two World Wars and again in post-World War II America, Mises demonstrated a unique ability to attract intellectually creative students, thus fostering new generations of scholars to continue the ideas of the Austrian School of Economics.

Ludwig von Mises and the
Historical Context of His Time

An appreciation of Mises's defense of freedom requires an understanding of the political and ideological trends of the first half of the twentieth century. Throughout most of the nineteenth century, "liberalism" had meant belief in and devotion to personal freedom, constitutionally limited government, the sanctity of private property, as well as freedom of enterprise at home and free trade among the nations of the world.

But even before the First World War many of those who labeled themselves "liberals" were in fact advocates of what a few decades earlier, in prewar Imperial Germany, had been called "state socialism." For almost forty years before the First World War, many of the leading German economists, historians, and political scientists—who became widely known as members of the German Historical School—had argued that the socialists had been correct in their criticisms of free market capitalism. The unregulated market, they said, resulted in the exploitation of workers and a disregard of the "national interest." Where the socialists had gone wrong, they insisted, was in their radical demand for a revolutionary overthrow of the entire existing social order.

What Germany needed instead, they stated, was "state socialism," under which social reforms would be introduced to ameliorate the supposed "excesses" of unbridled laissez-faire. The German Historical School supported and encouraged the imposition of the modern welfare state by the German "Iron Chancellor," Otto von Bismarck, in the 1880s and 1890s. Socialized medicine, state-managed old-age pensions, minimum-wage laws, and government-sponsored public housing and recreational facilities would provide "cradle to grave" security for the "working classes," and would thus lure them away from the more radical proposals of the Marxian socialists.[5]

At the same time, government regulation of industry and agriculture through tariffs, cartels, and subsidies, as well as production and price controls, would assure that the activities of the "capitalist class" would be harnessed to what the political authorities considered to be in the "national interest." Pragmatism and expediency in all economic and social policy decisions were hailed as the highest forms of political wisdom and "statesmanship," in place of "inflexible" constitutional restraints that limited the discretionary power for government intervention.

Members of the German Historical School argued that old-fashioned classical liberalism had been purely "negative" in its understanding of freedom and in advocating that government's role was simply to secure the lives, liberty, and property of the citizenry from violence, aggression, and fraud. Government, they said, had to be more "positive" and active in providing social safety nets for the masses against the uncertainties of life. Hence, they and their "progressive" followers in England, France, and especially the United States soon were referring to their ideas as a newer and more enlightened "liberalism," which would create a truer and more complete "freedom" from want and worry.[6] The concept of liberalism, most particularly in the United States, was changing from a political and economic philosophy of individual liberty and free enterprise under the rule of law and limited government to a notion of political paternalism with an increasingly intrusive hand of government in the social and commercial affairs of its citizens.[7]

The last decades of the nineteenth century also saw the growth of two other modern forms of collectivism: socialism and nationalism. Their common premise was that the individual and his interests were always potentially in conflict with the best interests of society as a whole. The Marxists claimed to have discovered the inescapable "laws of history," which demonstrated that the emergence of the division of labor and private property split society into inherently antagonistic social "classes." Those who owned the means of production earned rent and profit by extracting a portion of the wealth produced by the nonowning workers whom the owners of productive property employed in agriculture and industry.

Eventually this class conflict would lead, through a process of historical evolution, to a radical and revolutionary change in which the workers would rise up and expropriate the property of the capitalists. After having socialized the means of production, the new workers' state would introduce central planning in place of the previous decentralized and profit-oriented production plans of the now expropriated capitalists. Socialist central planning, it was claimed, would generate a level of production and a rising standard of living far exceeding anything experienced during the "capitalist phase" of human history. This process would culminate in a "post-scarcity" world in which all of man's wants and wishes would be fully satisfied, with selfishness and greed abolished from the face of the earth.[8]

The proponents of aggressive nationalism argued that there was, indeed, an inherent conflict among men in the world.[9] This antagonism, however, was not based on social classes as the Marxian socialists defined them. Instead, these conflicts were between nations and national groups. Unfortunately, the nationalist ideologues said, individuals within nations often acted in ways inconsistent with the best interests of the nation to which they belonged. Thus the particular interests of businessmen, workers, and those in various professional groups had to be regulated and controlled for the furtherance of the greater national good. As a result, aggressive nationalism dovetailed quite harmoniously—especially, though certainly not exclusively, in Imperial Germany—with the interventionist and welfare-statist policies of state socialism and the newer "progressive" liberalism.

Commercial and military conflict between the nations of the world was inevitable in the eyes of these nationalists. The prosperity of any one nation could only come at the expense of other nations. Hence, the task of all national statesmen was to foster the power and triumph of their own national group through the conquest and impoverishment of others around the world. Since no nation would willingly accept its own political and material destruction, war was an inescapable aspect of the human condition. Militarism and the martial spirit were likewise hailed as both necessary and superior to the "individualistic" and "pacifistic" spirit of production and trade.[10]

The culmination of these collectivist tendencies was the outbreak of the First World War in 1914, an analysis of the causes and consequences of which Ludwig von Mises offered in his 1919 volume, *Nation, State, and Economy*.[11] The Great War, as it was called, not only brought forth the triumph of the nationalistic spirit; it also saw the imposition of various forms of socialist central planning as virtually all the belligerent nations either nationalized or thoroughly controlled private industry and agriculture in the name of the wartime national emergency. The governments at war also established welfare-statist rationing and regulation of all consumer production since the needs of total war required total state responsibility for the supposed well-being of entire populations.

Out of the ashes of the First World War there arose new totalitarian states, first with the establishment of a communist dictatorship in Russia following the Bolshevik Revolution of 1917 under Lenin's leadership, and then with the rise to power of Mussolini and his Fascist Party in Italy in 1922. Both the communists and the fascists rejected the ideas and the institutions of classical liberalism. Constitutional government, the rule of law, civil liberties, and economic freedom were declared by both variations on the collectivist theme as reactionary hindrances to the success of, respectively, the worker's state in Soviet Russia and national greatness in Fascist Italy. Both communism and fascism insisted that the individual needed to be "reeducated" and made to conform to the wider socialist or nationalist good. The individual was to be reduced to a cog in the machinery of the all-powerful and all-planning state.[12]

Germany's defeat in the war had resulted in political and economic chaos, which culminated in the disastrous hyperinflation of the early 1920s.[13] Many of the social and cultural anchors of German society were unhinged by the war and the inflation.[14] A growing number of Germans longed for a "Leader" to guide them out of the morass of political instability and economic hardship. In 1925, Mises analyzed these trends in Germany and concluded that they were leading the German people toward a "national socialism," instead of either classical liberalism or Marxian socialism.[15] Anticipating the triumph of Hitler and his National Socialist (Nazi) movement in 1933, Mises warned in 1926 that many Germans were "setting their hopes on the coming of the 'strong man'—the tyrant who will think for them and care for them."[16]

In later years, Mises emphasized that while the Marxists in the Soviet Union used the tools of central planning to culturally redesign a socialist "new man" through various methods of indoctrination and thought control, the National Socialists in Nazi Germany took this a step further with their scheme of centrally planning the racial breeding of a new "master race."[17]

Capitalism, Socialism, and Interventionism

This was the historical context in which Mises published some of his most important works in the period between the two World Wars: *Socialism* (1922), *Liberalism* (1927), and *Critique of Interventionism* (1929). The task he set for himself was to offer a radically different vision of man in society from that presented by the socialists, nationalists, and interventionists. In place of their starting premise of inescapable conflicts among men in terms of "social class," nationality and race, or narrow group interest, Mises insisted that reason and experience demonstrated that all men could associate in peace for their mutual material and cultural betterment. The key to this was an understanding and appreciation of the benefits of a division of labor. Through specialization and trade the human race has the capacity to lift itself up from both poverty and war.

Men become associates in a common process of social cooperation, instead of antagonists with each attempting to rule over and plunder the others. Indeed, all that we mean by modern civilization, and the material and cultural comforts and opportunities that it offers man, is due to the highly productive benefits and advantages made possible by a division of labor. Men participated in this associative collaboration in the arena of competitive market exchange.

The confusion, Mises pointed out, is the failure to view this cooperative social process from a longer-run perspective than the changing circumstances of everyday life. In the rivalries of the market, there are always some who earn profits and others who suffer losses in the interactive and competitive processes of supply and demand. But what needs to be understood is that these changes in the short-run fortunes of various participants in the division of labor are the method through which each participant is informed and nudged into either doing more of some things or less of others. This process brings about the necessary adjustment of society's productive activities in order to assure that they tend to match and reflect the market pattern of consumer demand.[18]

Of course, political force can be substituted for the "reward" of profits and the "punishment" of losses. However, the costs of this substitution are extremely high, Mises argued. First, men are less motivated to apply themselves with intelligence and industry when forced to work under the lash of servitude and compulsion, and thus society loses what their free efforts and invention might have produced.[19] Second, men are forced to conform to the values and goals of those in command, and thus they lose the liberty of following their own ends and purposes, with no certainty that those who rule over them know better what may give them happiness and meaning in life.

And, third, socialist central planning and political intervention in the market, respectively, abolish or distort the functioning of social cooperation. A sustained and extended system of specialization for mutual improvement is only possible under a unique set of social and economic institutions. Without private ownership in the means of production, the coordination of multitudes of individual activities in the division of labor is impossible. Indeed, Mises's analysis of the "impossibility" of a socialist order being able to match the efficiency and productivity of a free market economy was the basis for his international stature and reputation as one of the most original economists of his time, and was the centerpiece of his book on *Socialism*.[20]

Private ownership and competitive market exchange enable the formation of prices for both consumer goods and the factors of production, expressed in the common denominator of a medium of exchange—money. On the basis of these money prices, entrepreneurs can engage in economic calculation to determine the relative costs and profitability of alternative lines of production. Without these market-generated prices, there would be no rational way to allocate resources among their competing uses to assure that those goods most highly valued by the buying public were produced in the least costly and therefore most economical manner. Economic calculation, Mises demonstrated, guarantees that the scarce means available are utilized to best serve the ends of the members of society.

Such rationality in the use of means to satisfy ends is impossible in a comprehensive system of socialist central planning. How, Mises asked, will the socialist planners know the best uses for which the factors of production under their central control should be applied without such market-generated money prices? Without private ownership of the means of production there would be nothing (legally) to buy and sell. Without the ability to buy and sell, there will be no bids and offers, and therefore no haggling over terms of trade among competing buyers and sellers. Without the haggling of market competition there would, of course, be no agreed-upon terms of exchange. Without agreed-upon terms of exchange, there are no actual market prices. And without such market prices, how will the central planners know the opportunity costs and therefore the most highly valued uses for which those resources could or should be applied? With the abolition of private property, and therefore market exchange and prices, the central planners would lack the necessary institutional and informational tools to determine what to produce and how, in order to minimize waste and inefficiency.

Socialists and many nonsocialist economists claimed over the decades that Mises was "wrong," when he said that socialism was "impossible." They pointed to the Soviet Union and said it existed and operated. However in numerous places in his various writings, beginning from the early 1920s, Mises insisted that he was not saying that a socialist system could not exist. Of course, the factors of production could be nationalized and a central planning agency could be delegated the responsibility to direct all the production activities of the society.

But any supposed rationality and seeming degree of efficiency observed in the workings of the Soviet and similar socialist economies was due to the fact that such socialist planning systems existed in a world in which there were still functioning market societies. The existing market economies provided various "shadow prices" that the socialist planners could try to use as proxies and benchmarks for evaluating their own allocation and production decisions. However, since the actual economic circumstances in such a socialist economy would never be an exact duplicate of the conditions in the neighboring market societies—resources availabilities, labor skills, the quantity and qualities of capital equipment, the fertility and variety of land, the patterns of consumer demand—such proxy prices could never completely "solve" the economic calculation problem for the socialist planners in places like the Soviet Union.[21]

Therefore, Mises declared in 1931, "From the standpoint of both politics and history, this proof [of the "impossibility" of socialist planning] is certainly the most important discovery by economic theory.... It alone will enable future historians to understand how it came about that the victory of the socialist movement did not lead to the creation of the socialist order of society."[22]

At the same time, Mises demonstrated the inherent inconsistencies in any system of piecemeal political intervention in the market economy. Price controls and production restrictions on entrepreneurial decision-making bring about distortions and imbalances in the relationships of supply and demand, as well as constraints on the most efficient use of resources in the service of consumers. The political intervener is left with the choice of either introducing new controls and regulations in an attempt to compensate for the distortions and imbalances the prior interventions have caused, or repealing the interventionist controls and regulations already in place and allowing the market once again to be free and competitive. The path of one set of piecemeal interventions followed by another entails a logic of the growth of government that eventually would result in the entire economy coming under state management. Hence, interventionism consistently applied could lead to socialism on an incremental basis.[23]

The most pernicious form of government intervention, in Mises's view, was political control and manipulation of the monetary system. Contrary to both the Marxists and the Keynesians, Mises did not consider the fluctuations experienced over the business cycle to be an inherent and inescapable part of the free market economy. Waves of inflation and depression were the product of political intervention in money and banking. And this included the Great Depression of the 1930s, Mises argued.

Under various political and ideological pressures, governments had monopolized control over the monetary system. They used the ability to create money out of thin air through the printing press or on the ledger books of the banks to finance government deficits and to artificially lower interest rates to stimulate unsustainable investment booms. Such monetary expansions always tended to distort market prices resulting in misdirections of resources, including labor, and malinvestments of capital. The inflationary upswing that is caused by an artificial expansion of money and bank credit sets the stage for an eventual economic downturn. By distorting the rate of interest, the market price for borrowing and lending, the monetary authority throws savings and investment out of balance, with the need for an inevitable correction. The "depression" or "recession" phase of the business cycle occurs when the monetary authority either slows downs or stops any further increases in the money supply. The imbalances and distortions become visible, with some investment projects having to be written down or written off as losses, with reallocations of labor and other resources to alternative, more profitable employments, and sometimes significant adjustments and declines in wages and prices to bring supply and demand back into proper order.[24]

The Keynesian revolution of the 1930s, which then dominated economic policy discussions for decades following the Second World War, was based on a fundamental misconception of how the market economy worked, in Mises's view. What Keynes called "aggregate demand failures," to explain the reason for high and prolonged unemployment, distracted attention away from the real source of less than full employment: the failure of producers and workers on the "supply-side" of the market to price their products and labor services at levels that potential demanders would be willing to pay. Unemployment and idle resources were pricing problems, not demand management problems. Mises considered Keynesian economics basically to be nothing more than a rationale for special interest groups, such as trade unions, that didn't want to adapt to the reality of supply and demand and what the market viewed as their real worth.[25]

Thus Mises's conclusion from his analysis of socialism and interventionism, including monetary manipulation, was that there is no alternative to a thoroughgoing unhampered free market economy, and one that included a market-based monetary system, such as the gold standard.[26] Both socialism and interventionism are, respectively, unworkable and unstable substitutes for capitalism. The classical liberal defends private property and the free market economy, he insisted, precisely because it is the only system of social cooperation that provides wide latitude for freedom and personal choice to all members of society, while generating the institutional means for coordinating the actions of billions of people in the most economically rational manner.

Classical Liberalism, Freedom, and Democracy

Mises's defense of classical liberalism against these various forms of collectivism, however, was not limited to the "merely" economic benefits from the private-property order. Property also provides man with that most valuable and cherished object—*freedom*. Property gives the individual an arena of autonomy in which he may cultivate and live out his own conception of the good and meaningful life. It also protects him from dependency on the state for his existence; through his own efforts and voluntary exchange with other free men he is not beholden to any absolute political authority that would dictate the conditions of his life. Freedom and property, if they are to be secure, require *peace*. Violence and fraud must be outlawed if each man is to take full advantage of what his interests and talents suggest would be the most profitable avenues to achieve his goals in consensual association with others.

The classical-liberal ideal also emphasizes the importance of *equality before the law*, Mises explained. Only when political privilege and favoritism are eliminated can each man have the latitude to use his own knowledge and talents in ways that benefit himself and also rebound, through the voluntary transactions of the market, to the betterment of society as a whole. This means, at the same time, that a liberal society is one that accepts that *inequality of income and wealth* is inseparable from individual freedom. Given the diversity of men's natural and acquired abilities and volitional inclinations, the rewards earned by people in the marketplace will inevitably be uneven. Nor can it be otherwise if we are not to diminish or even suffocate the incentives that move men to apply themselves in creative and productive ways.

The role of government, therefore, in the classical-liberal society is to respect and protect each individual's right to his life, liberty, and property. The significance of *democracy*, in Mises's view, is not that majorities are always right or should be unrestrained in what they may do to minorities through the use of political power. Elected and representative government is a means of changing those who hold political office without resort to revolution or civil war. It is an institutional device for maintaining social peace. It was clear to Mises from the experience of communism and fascism, as well as from the many tyrannies of the past, that without democracy the questions of who shall rule, for how long, and for what purpose would be reduced to brute force and dictatorial power. Reason and persuasion should be the methods that men use in their dealings with one another—both in the marketplace and the social and political arenas—and not the bullet and the bayonet.[27]

In his book on classical liberalism, Mises bemoaned the fact that people are all too willing to resort to state power to impose their views of personal conduct and morality whenever their fellow human beings veer from their own conception of the "good," the "virtuous," and the "right." He despaired, "The propensity of our contemporaries to demand authoritarian prohibition as soon as something does not please them...shows how deeply ingrained the spirit of servility still remains in them.... A free man must be able to endure it when his fellow men act and live otherwise than he considers proper. He must free himself from the habit, just as soon as something does not please him, of calling for the police"[28]

What, then, should guide social policy in determining the limits of government action? Mises was a utilitarian who argued that laws and institutions should be judged by the standard of whether and to what extent they further the goal of peaceful social cooperation. Society is the most important means through which men are able to pursue the ends and purposes that give meaning to their lives. But Mises was not what has become known in philosophical discussion as an "act-utilitarian," that is, one who believes that a course of action or a policy is to be determined on an ad hoc, case-by-case basis. Rather, he was a "rule-utilitarian," that is, one who believes that any particular course of action or policy must be evaluated in terms of its consistency with general rules of personal and social conduct that reason and experience have accumulated as guides to conduct. Any action's long-run influences and consequences must be taken into consideration in terms of its consistency with and relationship to the preservation of the institutions essential for successful social interaction.[29] This is the meaning of the phrase Mises often used: the "rightly understood long-run interests" of the members of society.[30]

Thus his defense of democracy and constitutional limits on the powers of government was based on the reasoned judgment that history has demonstrated far too many times that the resort to nondemocratic and "extra-constitutional" means has led to violence, repression, abrogation of civil and economic liberties, and a breakdown of respect for law and the legal order, which destroys the long-run stability of society. The apparent "gains" and "benefits" from "strong men" and "emergency measures" in times of seeming crisis have always tended to generate "costs" and "losses" of liberty and prosperity in the longer run that more than exceed the supposed "short-run" stability, order, and security promised by such methods.

Classical Liberalism and International Peace

The benefits from social cooperation through a market-based division of labor, Mises argued, are not limited to a country's borders. The gains from trade through specialization extend to all corners of the globe. Hence, the classical-liberal ideal is inherently cosmopolitan. Aggressive nationalism, in Mises's view, not only threatens to bring death and destruction through war and conquest, it also denies all men the opportunity to benefit from productive intercourse by imposing trade barriers and various other restrictions on the free movement of goods, capital, and people from one country to another. Prosperity and progress are artificially constrained within national boundaries. This perversely can create the conditions for war and conquest as some nations conclude that the only way to obtain the goods and resources available in another country is through invasion and violence. Eliminate all trade barriers and restrictions on the free movement of goods, capital, and men, and limit governments to the securing of each individual's life, liberty, and property, and most of the motives and tensions that can lead to war will have been removed.

Mises also suggested that many of the bases for civil wars and ethnic violence would be removed if the right of self-determination were recognized in determining the borders between countries. Mises took great care to explain that by "self-determination" he did not mean that all those belonging to a particular racial, ethnic, linguistic, or religious group are to be forced into the same nation-state. He clearly stated that he meant the right of individual self-determination through plebiscite. That is, if the individuals in a town or region or district vote to join another nation, or wish to form their own independent country, they should have the freedom to do so.

There still may be minorities within these towns, regions, or districts, of course, that would have preferred to remain part of the country to which they belonged, or would have preferred to join a different country. But however imperfect self-determination may be, it would at least potentially reduce a good amount of the ethnic, religious, or linguistic tensions. The only lasting solution, Mises said, is the reduction of government involvement to those limited classical-liberal functions, so the state may not be used to impose harm or disadvantage on any individual or group in society for the benefit of others.[31]

Classical Liberalism and the General Welfare

Finally, Mises also discussed this question: For whose benefit does the classical liberal speak in society? Unlike virtually all other political and ideological movements, liberalism is a social philosophy of the common good. Both at the time that Mises wrote many of his works and now, political movements and parties often resort to the rhetoric of the common good and the general welfare, but in fact their goals are to use the power of government to benefit some groups at the expense of others.

Government regulations, redistributive welfare programs, trade restrictions and subsidies, tax policies, and monetary manipulation are employed to grant profit and employment privileges to special-interest groups that desire positions in society they are unable to attain on the open, competitive market. Corruption, hypocrisy, and disrespect for the law, as well as abridgements on the freedom of others, naturally follow from this.

What liberalism offers as an ideal and as a goal of public policy, Mises declared, is an equality of individual rights for all under the rule of law, with privileges and favors for none. It speaks for and defends the freedom of each individual and therefore is the voice of liberty for all. It wants every person to be free to apply himself in the pursuit of his own goals and purposes, so he and others can benefit from his talents and abilities through the peaceful transactions of market exchange. Classical liberalism wants elimination of government intervention in human affairs, so political power is not abusively applied at the expense of anyone in society.[32]

Mises was not unaware of the power of special-interest–group politics and the difficulty of opposing the concentrated influence of such groups in the halls of political power.[33] But he insisted that the ultimate power in society resides in the power of ideas. Ideas are what move men to action, that make them bare their chests at barricades, or that embolden them to oppose wrongheaded policies and resist even the strongest of vested interests. Ideas are what have achieved all the victories that have been won by freedom over the centuries.

Neither political deception nor ideological compromise can win liberty in the twenty-first century. Only the power of ideas, clearly stated and forthrightly presented, can do so. And that is what stands out in Mises's books and makes them enduring sources of the case for freedom.

When Mises wrote many of his books in the 1920s, 1930s, and 1940s—communism and fascism seemed irresistible forces in the world.

Since then, their ideological fire has been extinguished in the reality of what they created and the unwillingness of tens of millions to live under their yoke. Nonetheless, many of their criticisms of the free market continue to serve as rationales for the intrusions of the interventionist welfare state in every corner of society. Many of the contemporary arguments against "globalization" often resemble the criticisms leveled against free markets and free trade by European nationalists and socialists of one hundred years ago.[34]

Mises's arguments for individual freedom and the market economy in the pages of *Socialism, Liberalism, Critique of Interventionism, Omnipotent Government, Bureaucracy, Planned Chaos, Human Action,* and many others continue to ring true and remain relevant to our own times. It is what makes his works as important now as when he wrote them across the decades of the twentieth century.

Notes

[1]On Mises's life and contributions to economics and the philosophy of freedom, see Richard M. Ebeling, *Austrian Economics and the Political Economy of Freedom* (Northampton, MA: Edward Elgar, 2003), chap. 3, "A Rational Economist in an Irrational Age: Ludwig von Mises," pp. 61–99; and Richard M. Ebeling, "Planning for Freedom: Ludwig von Mises as Political Economist and Policy Analyst" in Richard M. Ebeling, ed., *Competition or Compulsion: The Market Economy versus the New Social Engineering* (Hillsdale, MI: Hillsdale College Press, 2001), pp. 1–85; see also Murray N. Rothbard, *Ludwig von Mises: Scholar, Creator, Hero* (Auburn, AL: Ludwig von Mises Institute, 1988), and Israel M. Kirzner, *Ludwig von Mises* (Wilmington, DE: ISI Books, 2001).

[2]On Mises's family background and the cultural climate of Vienna and Austria in terms of the Jews and anti-Semitism, see Richard M. Ebeling, "Ludwig von Mises and the Vienna of His Time," Parts I & II, *The Freeman* (March & April 2005): 24–31 & 19–25.

[3]On Mises's work as policy analyst and advocate in the Austria of the interwar period, see Richard M. Ebeling, "The Economist as the Historian of Decline: Ludwig von Mises and the Austria Between the Two World Wars" in Richard M. Ebeling, ed., *Globalization: Will Freedom or Global Government Dominate the International Marketplace* (Hillsdale, MI: Hillsdale College Press, 2002), pp. 1–68.

[4]Ludwig von Mises, *Human Action: A Treatise on Economics* [1949] (Irvington-on-Hudson, NY: Foundation for Economic Education, [3ʳᵈ rev. ed., 1966] 1996).

[5]Bismarck told an American admirer, "My idea was to bribe the working class, or shall I say, to win them over, to regard the state as a social institution existing for their sake and interested in their welfare." See William H. Dawson, *The Evolution of Modern Germany*, Vol. II (New York: Charles Scribner's Sons, 1914), p. 349.

[6]On the ideas and development of the German welfare state and regulated economy in the late nineteenth and early twentieth centuries, see Ebeling, *Austrian Economics and the Political Economy of Freedom*, chap. 7, "The Political Myths and Economic Realities of the Welfare State," pp. 179–202, especially pp. 179–84; and Richard M. Ebeling, "National Health Care and the Welfare State," in Jacob G. Hornberger and Richard M. Ebeling, eds., *The Dangers of Socialized Medicine* (Fairfax, VA: The Future of Freedom Foundation, 1994), pp. 25–37; see also Mises's criticisms of the German Historical School in "The Historical Setting of the Austrian School of Economics" [1969], reprinted in Bettina Bien Greaves, ed., *Austrian Economics: An Anthology* (Irvington-on-Hudson, NY: Foundation for Economic Education, 1996), pp. 53–76, especially pp. 60–69.

[7]See Richard M. Ebeling, "Free Markets, the Rule of Law, and Classical Liberalism," *The Freeman* (May 2004): 8–15.

[8]Ludwig von Mises showed the inherent flaws and contradictions in the Marxian theory of history and class conflict in *Socialism: An Economic and Sociological Analysis* (Indianapolis, IN: Liberty Classics, 1981 [1922; rev. eds., 1932, 1951]), pp. 279–320; and *Theory and History: An Interpretation of Social and Economic Evolution* (Indianapolis, IN: Liberty Fund, 2005 [1957]), pp. 102–58.

[9]On the evolution and meanings of nationality and nationalism, see Carlton J. H. Hayes, *The Historical Evolution of Modern Nationalism* (New York: Richard R. Smith, 1931); Hayes, *Essays on Nationalism* (New York: Macmillan, 1928); Walter Sulzbach, *National Consciousness* (Washington, DC: American Council on Public Affairs, 1943); and Frederick Hertz, *Nationality in History and Politics* (New York: Oxford University Press, 1944).

[10]Ludwig von Mises, "Autarky and Its Consequences" [1943] in Richard M. Ebeling, ed., *Money, Method and the Market Process: Essays by Ludwig von Mises* (Norwell, MA: Kluwer Academic Press, 1990), p. 138: "Aggressive or militaristic nationalism aims at conquest and the subjugation of other nations by arms. Economic Nationalism aims at the furthering the well-being of one's own nation or some of its groups through inflicting harm upon foreigners by economic measures, for instance: trade and migration barriers, expropriation of foreign investments, repudiation of foreign debts, currency devaluation, and foreign exchange control."

[11]Ludwig von Mises, *Nation, State, and Economy: Contributions to the Politics and History of Our Time* (New York: New York University Press, 1983 [1919]).

[12]See Richard M. Ebeling, *Austrian Economics and the Political Economy of Freedom*, chap. 6, "Classical Liberalism and Collectivism in the 20th Century," pp. 159–78, especially pp. 159–63; on the political and ideological similarities of communism, fascism, and Nazism, see Ludwig von Mises, *Planned Chaos* (Irvington-on-Hudson, NY: Foundation for Economic Education, 1947), pp. 62–79; see also Richard Overy, *The Dictators:*

Hitler's Germany, Stalin's Russia (New York: W. W. Norton, 2004); A. James Gregor, *The Faces of Janus: Marxism and Fascism in the Twentieth Century* (New Haven, CT: Yale University Press, 2000); and Francois Furet, *The Passing of an Illusion: The Idea of Communism in the Twentieth Century* (Chicago: University of Chicago Press, 1999); and Richard Pipes, *Russia Under the Bolshevik Regime* (New York: Alfred A. Knopf, 1993), pp. 240–81.

[13] For Mises's analysis of the Great German Inflation, see his monograph, "Stabilization of the Monetary Unit—From the Viewpoint of Theory" [1923], in Percy L. Greaves, ed., *Ludwig von Mises, On the Manipulation of Money and Credit* (Dobbs Ferry, NY: Free Market Books, 1978), pp. 1–49, and Ludwig von Mises, "Business Under German Inflation" [1946], reprinted in *Ideas on Liberty* (November 2003): 10–13; see also Richard M. Ebeling, "The Great German Inflation," *Ideas on Liberty* (November 2003): 4–5.

[14] See Albrecht Mendelssohn Bartholdy, *The War and German Society: The Testament of a Liberal* (New York: Howard Fertig, 1971 [1937]), and Mortiz J. Bonn, *Wandering Scholar* (London: Cohen & West, Ltd., 1949), pp. 273–90.

[15] Ludwig von Mises, "Anti-Marxism" [1925] in *Critique of Interventionism* (Irvington-on-Hudson, NY: Foundation for Economic Education, 1996 [1929]), pp. 71–95.

[16] Ludwig von Mises, "Social Liberalism," [1926] in *Critique of Interventionism*, p. 67.

[17] Mises, *Planned Chaos*, pp. 77–78.

[18] Mises, *Socialism*, pp. 256–78; *Human Action*, pp. 143–76.

[19] Mises, *Human Action*, pp. 628–34.

[20] Ludwig von Mises, "Economic Calculation in the Socialist Commonwealth" [1920], in F. A. Hayek, *Collectivist Economic Planning: Critical Studies on the Possibilities of Socialism* (London: George Routledge & Sons, 1935), pp. 87–130, reprinted in Israel M. Kirzner, ed., *Classics in Austrian Economics: A Sampling in the History of a Tradition*, Vol. 3 (London: William Pickering, 1994), pp. 3–30, and Mises, *Socialism*, pp. 95–194; *Bureaucracy* (New Haven, CT: Yale University Press, 1944), pp. 20–56; *Human Action*, pp. 689–715; see also Richard M. Ebeling, "Why Socialism is 'Impossible,'" *The Freeman* (October 2004): 8–12.

[21] Ludwig von Mises, *Socialism*, p. 102; *Liberalism: The Classical Tradition* (Irvington-on-Hudson, NY: Foundation for Economic Education, [1927] 1996), p. 74; *Omnipotent Government*, p. 55; *Bureaucracy*, pp. 58–59; *Planned Chaos*, p. 84; *Human Action*, pp. 258–59 & 702–3.

[22] Ludwig von Mises, "On the Development of the Subjective Theory of Value" [1931] in *Epistemological Problems of Economics* [1933] (New York: New York University Press, 1981), p. 157.

[23] Mises, *Critique of Interventionism*, pp. 1–31 & 97–106; *Interventionism: An Economic Analysis* (Irvington-on-Hudson, NY: Foundation for Economic Education, 1996 [1941]); *Human Action*, pp. 716–79; *Planning for Freedom* (South Holland, IL: Libertarian Press, 4th ed., 1980 [1952]), pp. 1–49.

[24] Ludwig von Mises, *The Theory of Money and Credit* (Indianapolis, IN: Liberty Classics, 1981 [1912; rev. eds., 1934, 1953]); "Monetary Stabilization and Cyclical Policy"

[1928], reprinted in Kirzner, ed., *Classics in Austrian Economics*, Vol. 3, 33–111; *Human Action*, pp. 398–478, 538–86 & 780–803.

[25]For Mises's analysis of the causes and cures for the Great Depression, see Ludwig von Mises, "The Causes of the Economic Crisis" [1931] in Greaves, ed., *Ludwig von Mises, On the Manipulation of Money and Credit*, pp. 173–203; and on Keynesian Economics, see Mises, "Stones into Bread, The Keynesian Miracle" [1948] and "Lord Keynes and Say's Law" [1950] in *Planning for Freedom*, pp. 50–71; for a detailed comparison of the Austrian and Keynesian analyses of the Great Depression, see Richard M. Ebeling, "The Austrian Economists and the Keynesian Revolution: The Great Depression and the Economics of the Short-Run" in Richard M, Ebeling, ed., *Human Action: A 50-Year Tribute* (Hillsdale, MI: Hillsdale College Press, 2000), pp. 15–110.

[26]See Ebeling, *Austrian Economics and the Political Economy of Freedom*, chap. 5, "Ludwig von Mises and the Gold Standard," pp. 136–58.

[27]Mises, *Socialism*, pp. 58–73; *Liberalism*, pp. 18–42; *Human Action*, pp. 150–53 & 264–89

[28]Mises, *Liberalism*, p. 55.

[29]Mises, *Human Action*, pp. 664–88; *Theory and History*, pp. 44–61; and Henry Hazlitt, *The Foundations of Morality* (Irvington-on-Hudson, NY: Foundation for Economic Education, 1998 [1964]), pp. 55–61. See also Leland B. Yeager, *Ethics as Social Science: The Moral Philosophy of Social Cooperation* (Northampton, MA: Edward Elgar, 2001), pp. 81–97.

[30]Mises, *Human Action*, pp. 664–88.

[31]Mises, *Nation, State, and Economy*, pp. 31–56; *Liberalism*, pp. 105–21; *Omnipotent Government*, pp. 79–93.

[32]Mises, *Liberalism*, pp. 155–87.

[33]See, for example, his essay "The Clash of Group Interests" [1945], reprinted in Ebeling, ed., *Money, Method and the Market Process*, pp. 202–14.

[34]See Jerry Z. Muller, *The Mind and the Market: Capitalism in Modern European Thought* (New York: Alfred A. Knopf, 2002), and Ian Buruma and Avishai Margalit, *Occidentalism: The West in the Eyes of Its Enemies* (New York: The Penguin Press, 2004).

ROBERT SKIDELSKY

John Maynard Keynes: Founder of Macroeconomics

I. Keynes, Hayek, and Friedman

Any evaluation of John Maynard Keynes today is inescapably bound up with the question of what remains of Keynesian economics. Keynes was the first in the field of the three great twentieth-century economists—the other two being F. A. Hayek and Milton Friedman—and his contribution has to some extent been eclipsed by theirs. Today there is a tendency to think of Keynes's "general theory" (GT) as the theory of a deep slump, irrelevant to more "normal" times. This begs the question of the role of Keynesian economics in keeping times "normal." It is certainly arguable that both in 1987 and 2001 heavy deficit finance—the famous "economic stimulus"—warded off depressions. Keynesian attitudes are so built into our system of economic management, we no longer think of them as Keynesian.

There is the interesting question of the relationship between Keynes, Friedman, and Hayek. Friedman is often portrayed as the arch anti-Keynesian, but this is nonsense. In technical economics, monetarism and Keynesianism are first cousins—not surprising since Keynes started his professional career as a monetarist. Both are about the study of aggregates, that is, they are part of macroeconomics, which Hayek never accepted. In his technical economics Friedman is more Keynesian than Hayekian. In his political economy he is closer to Hayek. Both share a mistrust of government and faith in the market system. Friedman's faith in the market is more firmly rooted than is

Hayek's in neoclassical equilibrium theory. Hayek's position seems to have been that, even though market outcomes fall short of ideal equilibrium, government intervention will only make matters worse. His greatest contribution to economics was his depiction of the market as a discovery mechanism. Keynes would certainly have agreed with this as a long-run proposition, but would have added that we need a theory of short-run statesmanship to make the long run tolerable. Thus the connections and continuities between the three great economists are as striking as their differences, and we should avoid playing the competitive game with their reputations. The political economy we practice has been profoundly influenced by all three.

II. A Brief Biography

John Maynard Keynes was born at 6 Harvey Road, Cambridge, England, on 5 June 1883, into an academic family. He was the eldest son of John Neville Keynes, a logician and economist, and Florence Ada Brown, the daughter of a Congregational divine. He had an outstandingly successful school career at Eton College, which was followed by an equally glittering undergraduate one at King's College, Cambridge. There he gained a first-class honors degree in Mathematics, wrote papers on the medieval theologian Peter Abelard and the Conservative political philosopher Edmund Burke, and became President of the Cambridge Union and the University Liberal Club. Of crucial importance to his intellectual and moral formation was his election, in 1902, to the Cambridge Apostles, an exclusive "conversation" society, where he fell under the influence of the philosopher G. E. Moore, and which brought him the friendship of Lytton Strachey. Moore's *Principia Ethica* remained his "religion under the surface" for the rest of his life. It taught that the highest forms of civilized life were friendship, aesthetic enjoyments, and the pursuit of truth.

In 1906 Keynes was placed second in the Civil Service Examination, his worst marks being in economics, which he had studied briefly under Alfred Marshall. After two years in the India Office, in which he wrote a thesis on probability in his spare time, he started lecturing on monetary economics at Cambridge; in 1909, his thesis won him a fellowship at King's College, which remained his academic home for the rest of his life. His membership in the Bloomsbury Group, a commune of Cambridge-connected writers and painters who lived in the Bloomsbury district of London, dates from the start of his friendship with the painter Duncan Grant, Lyttton Strachey's cousin, in 1908. In 1913 he published his first book, *Indian Currency and Finance*, and served on the Royal Commission on Indian Finance and Currency.

Keynes helped to avert the collapse of the gold standard in the banking crisis of August 1914 that accompanied the outbreak of the First World War. From January 1915 to June 1919 he was a temporary civil servant at the Treasury, showing a notable ability to apply economic theory to the practical problems of war finance. He was against military conscription, and would have been a conscientious objector had his Treasury work not exempted him from military service. When Lloyd George succeeded Asquith as Prime Minister, Keynes (in January 1917) became head of the Treasury's new "A" Division, set up to manage external finance. He helped to build up the system of Allied purchases in neutral markets, while chafing at Britain's growing dependence on American loans and the failure to arrange a compromise peace. Keynes was chief Treasury representative at the Paris Peace Conference in 1919, where he tried unavailingly to limit Germany's bill for reparations, and to promote an American loan for the reconstruction of Europe. His resignation from the Treasury on 5 June 1919 was followed in December by the publication of *The Economic Consequences of the Peace*, the book that first brought him international fame. A bitter polemic, informed by both moral passion and economic argument, against the Allied policy of trying to extort from Germany an indemnity it could not pay, it reflected his revulsion against Lloyd George's leadership in both war and peace, and his fears for the future of European civilization. Unless the Versailles Treaty were drastically revised, "vengeance, I dare predict, will not limp."[1]

Between the wars, Keynes's life was divided among Cambridge, London, and East Sussex. He was a spectacularly successful investment bursar of King's College, and, despite some major reverses, made about £400,000 for himself over his lifetime—£12,000,000 (or $22,500,000 in today's currencies)—out of which he financed a fine collection of pictures and rare books and the building of the Cambridge Arts Theatre in 1935. In London, where he rented a house at 46 Gordon Square, he was, at various times, on the boards of five investment and insurance companies, the chief one being the National Mutual Life Assurance Company, which he chaired from 1921 to 1937. Between 1923 and 1931 he was chief proprietor and chairman of the board of the weekly journal *Nation and Athenaeum*, contributing regular articles on financial and economic topics. (He remained chairman of the board of the *New Statesman and Athenaeum* when the two journals merged in 1931.) Between 1911 and 1945, he edited the *Economic Journal*. In the 1920s his ideas on economic policy permeated Whitehall through monthly meetings of the Tuesday Club, a dining club started by his friend and stockbroker, Oswald Falk. In the 1930s, he sought to influence policy through his membership in the Prime Minister's Economic Advisory Council. In 1925, he took the lease of Tilton, a farmhouse in East Sussex, next door to Charleston, where Duncan Grant lived with the painter Vanessa Bell. This move coincided with his marriage to the Russian ballerina, Lydia Lopokova, who gave his life the emotional stability it had previously lacked, and which provided the necessary background for sustained intellectual effort.

In the 1920s, the postwar European inflations, succeeded in Britain by heavy unemployment, formed the background to his two theoretical books, *A Tract on Monetary Reform* (1923) and *A Treatise on Money* (1930), which dealt with the causes and consequences of monetary instability and their remedies. These theoretical exercises were punctuated by two notable polemical pamphlets, "The Economic Consequences of Mr. Churchill" (1925) and "Can Lloyd George Do It?" (1929), the second written with Hubert Henderson. The first attacked Churchill's decision, as Chancellor of the Exchequer, to put the pound back on the gold standard at an overvalued exchange rate against the dollar; the second was a plea for a large public works program. Reconciled to Lloyd George in 1926, Keynes attempted to provide the Liberal Party with a social philosophy of the "middle way" between individualism and state socialism, suitable for an inflexible industrial structure. Regulation of demand, he would later write, was the only way to maintain capitalism in conditions of freedom.[2]

The Great Depression of 1929–1932, together with technical flaws in *A Treatise on Money*, took Keynes back to the theoretical drawing board. What now seemed to be needed was not an explanation of Britain's "special problem" of persisting unemployment, but an explanation of how aggregate output could collapse, labor remain unused, and global depression persist in a world in which resources remained scarce. From the autumn of 1931 to the summer of 1935, Keynes worked on a new book of theory, initially titled "The Monetary Theory of Production." He was helped not just by older economists like Ralph Hawtrey and Dennis Robertson, but by Roy Harrod and a "Cambridge Circus" of young disciples led by Richard Kahn. There was just one major pamphlet in these years—"The Means to Prosperity"—written in June 1933. On a trip to the United States in 1934 to study the New Deal firsthand, he wrote: "Here, not in Moscow, is the economic laboratory of the world."

The General Theory of Employment, Interest and Money, published in February 1936, tried to demonstrate both that "underemployment equilibrium" was logically possible and how monetary "fine-tuning" by the central bank combined with an extensive "socialization" of investment could maintain full employment. The first proposition in particular divided the economics profession, since it rejected the "classical" thesis of a self-equilibrating economy. The publication of *The General Theory* confirmed the breach between Keynes and his chief collaborators in the 1920s, Dennis Robertson and Hubert Henderson. At the same time it marked the birth of a "Keynesian school" of economics led by Richard Kahn and Joan Robinson at Cambridge, Roy Harrod and James Meade at Oxford, and Nicholas Kaldor at the London School of Economics. In the United States the *The General Theory* supplied the younger generation of (mainly Harvard-trained) economists with a theoretical rationale for the New Deal. Keynes himself joined in the fierce controversies that his book generated, even though he was severely incapacitated from May 1937 to March 1939 with heart disease. As another European war, and with it, the return to deficit-financed full employment, became increasingly likely, Keynes sought to win acceptance for his revolution by showing how the management of aggregate demand to avert depression could just as easily be used to contain inflation in a war economy.

The upshot was his pamphlet "How to Pay for the War" (1940), which won the approval of his arch-critic Friedrich Hayek and whose logic influenced Kingsley Wood's war budget of 1941. Restored to a semblance of health by his doctor, Janos Plesch, Keynes himself returned to the Treasury in August 1940 as an unpaid adviser to the Chancellor of the Exchequer, and remained its dominating force for the rest of his life. Elevated to the House of Lords as Baron Keynes of Tilton, his influence was felt in the Beveridge Report on Social Security in 1942 and in the Employment White Paper of 1944, which pledged the government to maintain a "high and stable level of employment" after the war. In 1942, Keynes became chairman of the Council for the Encouragement of Music and the Arts (CEMA), a wartime innovation that inaugurated permanent state patronage of the arts. It was transformed into the Arts Council of Great Britain shortly before he died.

The American demand that in return for Lend-Lease Britain scrap its imperial preference system after the war inspired Keynes to his last great constructive effort—his plan for an International Clearing Union (1942). This was designed to shift balance-of-payments adjustments from debtor to creditor countries so as to avoid the externally generated deflationary shocks that had spread depression under the gold standard. The Bretton Woods Agreement of 1944, which set up a system of fixed but adjustable exchange rates and two new institutions, the International Monetary Fund and the International Bank for Reconstruction and Development, fell short of Keynes's hopes. The abrupt U.S. cancellation of Lend-Lease in August 1945 led him to undertake the fifth of his six Treasury missions to the United States in an effort to secure an American grant or interest-free loan of $5,000,000,000. Forced to accept a semicommercial loan for $3,750,000, Keynes gave a brilliant defense of his policy in his last speech to the House of Lords on 7 December 1945.

On 21 April 1946, worn out by his labors, he suffered a fatal heart attack at Tilton, a little short of his sixty-third birthday. In an imposing memorial service at Westminster Abbey, British Prime Minister Clement Attlee headed a list of mourners drawn from all walks of life.

III. Keynes's Major Contributions

To understand Keynes's contribution to economics, we need to say a word about how economics was done before Keynes. The "classical" theory, which Keynes set out to overthrow, was essentially the theory of a barter-exchange economy, in which Say's Law (that supply creates its own demand) held, and in which money affected only the price level. This barter-exchange model of the economy evolved into the timeless equilibrium models of Menger and Walras, in which everything depended on everything else simultaneously, so that their economics consisted of an infinitely extensible system of simultaneous equations. In these systems, prices, including wages, were infinitely flexible and markets always cleared. This kind of analysis was becoming common when Keynes started doing economics, and it has gained immeasurably as economics has become more mathematicized, eventually marginalizing the Keynesian approach within economic theory, though not in policy.

What led Keynes to challenge this way of doing economics?

First, I would put the influence of Alfred Marshall at Cambridge. Marshall was a kind of bridge between classical and neoclassical economics. He believed that the chief problem in economics was how to model time, and he developed the idea of three periods—the short run, the normal, and the long run—to explain how economies moved through time to adjust to shifts in supply and demand conditions. This was sharply different from the market-clearing simultaneity of the general equilibrium approach. His favorite form of analysis was partial equilibrium—dealing with the economy sector by sector and holding the rest of the system constant as he did so. Also he believed that money altered the economy, and that boom and slump entered the picture through the influence of money on prices. The Keynesian model is best seen through Marshallian spectacles—as a "temporary" or "short-period" equilibrium, with a fuller adjustment coming later, though with no tendency for adjustment to full employment.

Second, Keynes's training in economics was quite limited. In the preface to *The General Theory* he talked of the difficulty of escaping from old ideas "which ramify . . . into every corner of our minds." But Keynes didn't have to unlearn as much as some of his contemporaries. What he knew best was the theory of money, both pure and applied, which he taught in his prewar courses at Cambridge. The theory of value, based on the barter-exchange economy, ramified much less extensively. Unlike Hayek, he always viewed the economy from what would now be called a macroeconomic perspective. The whole struggle of his economics was to link up the inherited theory of money with a theory of output in order to explain fluctuations in the latter.

Third, his understanding of economics was strongly rooted in personal experience of financial markets. This was an interest from an early age. His credo was realism of assumptions, and he had no interest in working with models that had no reference to acknowledged facts. "Economics," he wrote in 1938, "is a science of thinking in terms of models joined to the art of choosing models which are relevant to the contemporary world.... Good economists are scarce because the gift for using "vigilant observation" to choose good models, although it does not require a highly specialized intellectual technique, appears to be a very rare one."[3] It was the experience of trying to work with one such model, the Quantity Theory of Money (QTM), which excluded by assumption the phenomena he sought to explain—fluctuations in output—that led him to develop a theory of output.

Finally, his experience working with the QTM led Keynes to insist that assumptions should be consistent with policy. Most economists tacitly abandoned their assumptions when endorsing remedies for slump conditions. Keynes set out to develop a model that justified a certain kind of intervention.

Keeping this in mind, we can group Keynes's main contributions to economics under three heads: the theory of deep economic fluctuations; the theory of effective demand; and the technique of stabilization policy based on the second.

The Theory of Economic Fluctuations

This cannot be wholly understood apart from Keynes's distinctive theory of probability, expounded in his *Treatise on Probability* (1921). As he was later to do in economics, he produced a "general theory" of probability, in which statistically based probability—as in insurance markets—was a "special case" of a logical theory of probability. This led him to distinguish between risk, or situations with known probability distributions, and uncertainty, when "there is no scientific basis on which to form any calculable probability." Much of economic life inhabited the second sphere, which is why booms and slumps were endemic. He wrote in 1937: "Thus the fact that our knowledge of the future is fluctuating, vague and uncertain, renders wealth a peculiarly unsuitable subject for the methods of the classical economic theory."[4] This may be contrasted with the modern mainstream view that agents maximize with known probability distributions, so that market-clearing models are the most appropriate for analyzing economic behavior. Keynes himself identified as a tacit axiom of the classical theory of the self-regulating economy that "at any given time facts and expectations were . . . given in a definite and calculable form."[5]

Keynes's theoretical work in the 1920s is devoted to unpackaging the Quantity Theory of Money, which ruled out, by assumption, the possibility that monetary disturbances can have "real" effects on the economy. This might be true in the long-run, Keynes remarked acidly, "but in the long-run we are all dead."[6] Keynes used the quantity of money *equation* to show that changes in the quantity of money can unsettle business expectations and the distribution of income, thereby causing short-run fluctuations in the level of business activity. In doing so, he emphasized the use of money as a "store of value" or hedge against uncertainty, and the distinction between fixed and flexible prices. In the *Treatise on Money*, he argued that the disturbing effects of money can arise not just from inflationary or deflationary policies, but from *autonomous* changes in business sentiment. Much of the *Treatise* is devoted to analyzing the consequences of short-run changes in the "propensity to hoard" or "velocity of circulation," which Keynes identifies, by means of his "Fundamental Equations," with the emergence of windfall profits and losses, and a disequilibrium between saving and investment. Keynes shows how disequilibrium prices produce an oscillation of boom and slump around a (notional) full-employment equilibrium. But such equilibrium is accidentally achieved, in the absence of appropriate monetary policy.

The chief theoretical point that emerges from these two works is the instability in what Keynes would later call the liquidity-preference schedule. His claim was that, in a variety of situations readily encountered in economic life, hoarding money can yield superior utility to investing it, and that this, combined with "sticky" wage and price contracts, can explain quite prolonged lapses from full employment. His contribution up to 1930 was largely a summation of the monetary theories of Irving Fisher and Knut Wicksell, and is properly regarded as a contribution to the theory of economic fluctuations, with increased emphasis on volatile expectations. Like Fisher, Keynes advocated a monetary policy of keeping domestic prices stable; this might be incompatible with adherence to the international gold standard, an institution that Keynes dismissed as a "barbarous relic."[7]

The Theory of Effective Demand

Keynes's revolutionary contribution to economics lies not in his theory of business fluctuations but in his theory of how aggregate output is determined. This is the subject matter of his *General Theory of Employment, Interest and Money* (1936). The QTM was a theory of the price level, when the levels of output and employment were explained in real, non-monetary terms. Following a suggestion from Ralph Hawtrey, Keynes agreed in 1930 that "it will probably be difficult in the future to prevent monetary theory and the theory of short-period supply from running together."[8] This was the start of Keynesian macroeconomics.

The core of *The General Theory* is the theory of effective demand. Its central claim is that aggregate supply and aggregate demand are reconciled through changes in quantities rather than prices. It is a short-period theory: Prices adjust only after, and as a result of, the fall in output and employment, and even then not completely. In the short-run, the volume of output in an economy is determined by the money demand for that output. The GT is the theory of what determines the level of money demand for output.

In Keynes's notation, $Y = C + I$. This tautology simply means that National Income (Y) is equal to the sum of the expenditure on National Output, divided into consumption spending (C) and investment spending (I). Consumption expenditure is governed by Keynes's "consumption function," based on the "psychological law" that consumption (and therefore saving, which is Y - C) is a stable fraction of total income, and that the marginal propensity to consume is less than unity. In a growing economy the gap between consumption and production must be filled by investment if full employment is to be maintained. The amount of investment is determined by the relationship between the expected profit rate ("marginal efficiency of capital") and the cost of borrowing (rate of interest). The rate of interest is the price of parting with money as determined by the state of liquidity preference. Thus given the interest rate, the amount of investment may fall short of what the community wishes to save. The revolutionary claim of the GT is that when this happens the divergent plans are brought into equality by a reduction in the level of income (output). Moreover, if the consumption function is known, it is possible to show, by a mathematical formula (Kahn's multiplier), by how much the community's income or alternatively employment must change to reconcile divergent saving and investment plans. The novelty of Keynes's treatment, as compared not just with the older theory, but his own *Treatise on Money*, was to demonstrate that an economy might be in equilibrium, with saving equal to investment, and aggregate demand equal to aggregate supply, at less than full employment.

Critics fastened on the most contentious feature of the new doctrine, the theory of "under-employment equilibrium." They denied that this was a genuine equilibrium; it was a disequilibrium state, frozen by the assumption that certain prices were fixed. Flexible prices would always ensure the desired level of employment, whatever was happening to aggregate money demand.

Keynes could have defended his position by saying that his fixed-price assumptions were realistic; but he set out to expose the logical flaws underlying the implicit classical price-adjustment story. He denied, first of all, that the interest rate was, or could be, determined in the market for saving and investment, since the quantity of saving depends on the level of current income. This was the basis of his view that changes in income equilibrate saving and investment plans.

As far as wage flexibility is concerned, Keynes agreed with the orthodox view that the *real* wage is inversely related to the quantity of employment, but denied that real wages are determined in the labor market by money-wage bargains, since an all-round reduction in money-wages might, by reducing the general price level, leave the real wage unaffected. The effect of a "flexible wages policy" thus depended entirely on its impact on the components of aggregate demand—consumption and investment—that might well be unfavorable.

Keynes conceded that, in time, the decline in employment (or money-wage rates) would, by decreasing the amount of money required to satisfy the business demand, lower the rate of interest required to satisfy the "propensity to hoard";[9] he also thought that after a slump a shortage of capital goods would develop that would revive profit expectations.[10] In short, a slump might eventually bring about the price adjustments that according to the classical economists were supposed to prevent the slump from occurring. He doubted, though, whether even longer-run forces would ensure a gravitational pull toward full employment. "We oscillate," he wrote, "round an intermediate position, appreciably below full employment and appreciably above the minimum employment a decline below which would endanger life."[11]

Despite nonacceptance by the leading economists of key elements in Keynes's macroeconomic model (Dennis Robertson, in particular, made a damaging attack on his theory of interest), critics were driven to argue for their positions within the analytical framework Keynes had set up. Macroeconomic analysis became part of the economists' tool kit, even if Keynes's own conclusions were rejected.

Let me try to grasp the vision or intuition that drives the technical analysis, but which is not perfectly captured by it. It is best revealed in answer to the question of why Keynes thought that full employment is unlikely to be the long-run, or normal, state of affairs. His answer is that the rate of interest tends to be permanently higher than the expected profit rate on capital, except in "moments of excitement." This is because money carries a permanent liquidity premium. Thus at almost any time the marginal return to money is greater than to capital goods, because money offers a unique hedge against uncertainty. Technically, there is zero or very low elasticity of substitution between money and goods. Over time, the marginal return to money falls less than the marginal return to goods. All wants are satiable except the desire for money. In this picture of the economy there is a permanent unemployment problem, because money employs no people in its production.

Notice, this would not be true under a *pure* gold standard in which the demand for liquidity would be satisfied by employing people to dig up gold. So we have two states of nature: pure metallic currency systems, which keep people poor but employed, and credit money systems, which enable societies to grow wealthier, but create semipermanent unemployment.

So we come back to the liquidity preference theory of the rate of interest, which is where Keynes's vision and theory meet. Keynes said that the rate of interest is the price people demand for parting with money. The only intelligible reason for demanding this price is uncertainty. With perfect information the classical theory of interest—as the price that savers demand of borrowers—would be true. Logically the equilibrating mechanism could be either income or interest, depending on the information assumption being used. To get Keynesian policy accepted it was enough to admit that the speculative demand for money balances to hold was normally greater than zero.

That subnormal activity is possible because of money's liquidity premium is a powerful intuition. But as a basis for a secure empirical generalization it is very shaky. Intuitively, one would expect the liquidity premium to be quite large at some times and quite small at others. Formally, that is all *General Theory* claims. Empirical data suggest that this is indeed the case, since, as Keynes himself recognized, there have been longish periods, such as the nineteenth century, when money's "own rate of interest" was sufficiently low to allow "a satisfactory average level of employment" under laissez-faire conditions.[12] Certainly there is little real warrant for Keynes's *obiter dictum* that modern societies achieve full employment only in "moments of excitement" when, as he put, "over-optimism triumphs over a rate of interest which, in a cooler light, would be seen to be excessive."[13] So although it would be wrong to call the General Theory the theory of a severe slump, there is little doubt that Keynes's gloomy vision owes a great deal to the Great Depression of 1929–1932.

Stabilization Technique

Keynes's three main theoretical books were aimed at providing justifications for conscious attempts to stabilize output and employment at a high level. The quest for output stabilization led directly to the development of National Income and Expenditure Accounts, to enable governments to estimate the size of the "output" gap—the gap between what the economy was producing and what it could produce at full employment (or, in later refinement, when it was growing to trend)—that needed to be plugged by extra spending. Keynes also insisted that the aggregate demand and supply framework of the General Theory could be used to work out how much spending needed to be withdrawn from an economy to prevent inflation if aggregate demand exceeded aggregate supply.

In principle, stabilization policy can be either monetary or fiscal, or some combination of both. In practice, Keynes rejected the monetary route to managing demand. He did not deny that investment was interest-elastic. But he thought that interest-rate changes, produced by varying the quantity of bank credit, were too slow-moving in their effects on investment; and he was worried that if interest rates were raised to check a boom it would be difficult to bring them down to check a slump, since the expectation of falling rates would increase the "propensity to hoard." So he advocated a policy of permanently cheap money, to be buttressed by capital controls if required. This left fiscal policy as the main instrument for preventing both slumps and inflationary booms. A shorthand description of Keynesian fiscal policy is that the budget should be balanced over the cycle, that is, government should incur debt during the downswing and accumulate surpluses in the upswing. It is not clear that Keynes ever thought this, or at least consistently. His final position rested on a distinction between current and capital expenditure. The "ordinary" budget should be permanently balanced (even in surplus); capital programs should be accelerated or retarded to deal with the cycle. This assumed that a large proportion of investment would be public investment. As he put it in 1943: "If two-thirds or three quarters of total investment is carried out or can be influenced by public or semi-public bodies, a long-term programme of a stable character should be capable of reducing the potential range of fluctuation to much narrower limits than formerly.... If this is successful it should not be too difficult to offset small fluctuations by expediting or retarding some items in this long-term programme."[14]

Finally, Keynes attached only minor importance to exchange-rate adjustments. His Clearing Union Plan (1942) provided for fixed, but adjustable, rates; this was a feature of the Bretton Woods Agreement (1944). Keynes's attitude—like that of most economists of his day—was governed by price-elasticity pessimism. He preferred countries to use, if necessary, capital controls to protect their balance of payments in the framework of a monetary regime of fixed exchange rates, low tariffs, and automatic creditor lending through international institutions.

Keynes was not an ivory-tower theorist. His theorizing was controlled by real world events. His own investment experience enabled him to identify the "speculative" motive for holding money; his sense of political fragility led him to concentrate on the economics of stabilization; his civil service experience enabled him to turn theories into workable plans. His economic theorizing was less directly, but still importantly, controlled by his philosophical beliefs, particularly by his conception of the good life and of the conditions of just exchange.

IV. The Legacy

Economics was transformed by its encounter with Keynes. Macroeconomics became for many years a dominant part of the subject; macroeconomic forecasting became the main tool of government policy. However, Keynes's doctrines never won universal acceptance, and key aspects of his theoretical and policy legacy have been challenged. The debated issues can be grouped under four headings.

Acceptance of Keynes's Theory

What Keynes bequeathed was not the same as what was accepted. The first theoretical breach came with demonstrations by Pigou (1942) and by Modigliani (1944) that the Keynesian slogan "quantities adjust, not prices" was true only if money wages were rigid. This became the basis of the "neoclassical synthesis," which grafted Keynesian macroeconomics onto classical theory, but left the rigidities unexplained. Milton Friedman's counterattack was both methodological and theoretical. On the one hand, he argued that it was not acceptable to posit *ad hoc* supply functions. Second, his own application of neoclassical standards of method to Keynes's aggregate equations—seen in his permanent income hypothesis (1957), the stable demand for money function (1956, 1963), and the theory of the "natural rate" of unemployment (1968)—undermined the case for Keynesian stabilization policy. Economies were more cylically stable than Keynes had supposed; multipliers were small, or nonexistent; government manipulation of aggregate demand had no permanent "real" effects, but only raised the inflation rate. These "policy ineffectiveness" propositions were to be hardened still further by the "rational expectations" school of Robert Lucas and Thomas Sargent. The tendency of Friedman's critique (popularly called "monetarism") was to reinsert an updated version of the Quantity Theory of Money into the heart of macroeconomics. It revived the pre-Keynesian notion (adumbrated by Keynes himself in the *Tract on Monetary Reform*) that the most important macroeconomic function of governments was to keep stable the purchasing power of money.

Acceptance of Keynesian Policy

Contrary to widespread mythology, this was patchy. Both the British and U.S. governments committed themselves to targeting "high" levels of employment, but it is often asserted that U.S. policy became Keynesian only in the early 1960s, and German policy became Keynesian in the late 1960s. Both episodes were fairly brief. Much of this discussion begs the question of what one means by "Keynesian" policy. Running a budget deficit is no more a sign of Keynesian virtue than running a budget surplus in boom conditions is anti-Keynesian. An alternative argument is that Keynes's influence was exerted not so much through national policies as through the willingness of the United States to provide the rest of the world with reserves and liquidity. However, this likewise begs the question of how "Keynesian" this willingness was.

The Impact of Policy on Events

For a long time, the canonical view was that Keynesian demand-management policies and Keynesian-inspired institutions (the Bretton

Woods system) were mainly responsible for the uniquely successful employment and growth performance of most countries in the 1950s and 1960s. Today most of the credit for that "golden age" is given to opportunities for "catching up" with American technology, recession-proof military spending by the United States, and high levels of "social" spending.

In the 1950s and 1960s it was common to argue that Keynesian policy helped to save capitalism by removing the scourge of mass unemployment. (In Marxist terms, it *legitimized* the capitalist order.) By the 1970s it was being argued that it endangered the long-run survival of capitalism by producing rising inflation, an expanding public sector, and increasingly draconian wage and price controls. Specifically, Keynesian fiscal philosophy, by justifying budget deficits in some circumstances, opened the way, in a democracy, to permanent deficit finance. Alternatively, the Keynesian policy of "fine-tuning" the economy was destabilizing, rather than stabilizing, owing to the existence of variable leads and lags. Keynesian uncertainty, that is, applied as much to Keynesian policy as to the operations of the market economy.

The Current Debate over Keynesian Economics

According to the monetarist-cum-rational expectations schools, Keynesian economics failed the predictive test: It led to "stagflation." In the 1970s, Keynesian policies were attacked for ignoring the existence of a "natural" rate of unemployment, and (by the Virginia or Public Choice school) for assuming that politicians wanted to maximize the collective social welfare, rather than their own individual utilities. Taken together, these two attacks offered a forceful argument against the use of discretionary fiscal and monetary policy to balance economies.

The use of models of economies with nominal rigidities is still general, but whether these rigidities are to be taken as given is much more questioned than in 1950s and 1960s. The dominant "supply-side revolution" of the 1980s was chiefly concerned to dissolve rigidities seen as institutional by deregulating labor markets. Against this, the "new Keynesians" explained how sticky prices are rational because of transactions and information costs, and how shocks to demand can destroy both physical and human capital. These explanations seemed both to strengthen and weaken the case for Keynesian macroeconomic policy. On the one hand, they gave renewed intellectual respectability to stabilization policy. On the other hand, by explicitly introducing inflation into their analyses, they conceded the existence of a rate of unemployment (the so-called NAIRU or Non-Inflation Accelerating Rate of Unemployment) below which unemployment could not be pushed by manipulating demand. Finally, against the mainstream profession's use of Bayesian statistics and decision theory to model agents' behavior, a minority school of "Post-Keynesians" continues to assert the fundamental nature of Keynes's attack on the rationality axiom.

An interim judgment on the Keynesian Revolution would be that the main body of classical economics was too well entrenched to be overthrown by the frontal assault he mounted. The notion that uncertainty was at the heart, rather than at the financial margins, of economic processes proved too subversive of the science economics claims to be acceptable. At the same time stabilization policy is widely accepted and practiced, in contradistinction to much of textbook theory. So Keynes's hope of an economic science whose assumptions are congruent with economic policy has yet to be realized. Many economists would say today of Keynes what Marshall said of Jevons: "His success was aided even by his faults . . . he led many to think he was correcting great errors; whereas he was really only adding very important explanations."[15] Whether this will be the final verdict is still questionable.

Notes

All references to Keynes's writing are to the *Collected Writings of John Maynard Keynes*, 30 volumes, published by Macmillan/Cambridge University Press for the Royal Economic Society, 1971–1989. Referred to below as *CW*.

[1]John Maynard Keynes, *The Economic Consequences of the Peace*, 1919, *CW*, p. 170.
[2]Keynes, *The General Theory of Employment, Interest and Money*, 1936, *CW* p. 381; "How to Pay for the War," 1940, *CW*, p. 123.
[3]Keynes to Roy Harrod, 4 July 1938, *CW*, pp. 296–97.
[4]Keynes, "The General Theory of Employment," *Quarterly Journal of Economics*, February 1937, *CW*, p. 113.
[5]Ibid., p. 112.

[6]Keynes, *A Tract on Monetary Reform*, 1923, *CW*, p. 65.
[7]Ibid., p. 138.
[8]Keynes to Hawtrey, 27 August 1930, *CW*, p. 146.
[9]Keynes, 1937, *CW*, p. 118.
[10]Keynes, *General Theory*, 1937, *CW*, pp. 317–18.
[11]Ibid., p. 254.
[12]Ibid., p. 307.
[13]Ibid., p. 322.
[14]Keynes, "The Long-Term Problem of Full Employment," 25 May 1943, *CW*, p. 322.
[15]A. Marshall, *Principles of Economics*, 8th ed. (London: Macmillan, 1920), p. 85.

Bibliography

Davidson, Paul. "Would Keynes be a New Keynesian?" *Eastern Economic Journal* 18(4): 1992.

Harrod, R. F. *The Life of John Maynard Keynes*. London: Macmillan, 1951.

Hicks, J. R. *The Crisis in Keynesian Economics*. Oxford: Basil Blackwell, 1974.

Keynes, John Maynard.
> *Activities 1939-1945: Internal War Finance*. 1940. *CW*, vol. xxii.
> *Activities 1940-1946 : Shaping the Post-War World*. 1943. *CW*, vol. xxvii.
> *The Economic Consequences of the Peace*. 1919. *CW*, vol. ii.
> "The Economic Consequences of Mr. Churchill." 1925. *CW*, vol. ix.
> *The General Theory and After: Part I Preparatio*. 1930. *CW*, vol. xiii.
> *The General Theory and After: Part II Defence and Development*. 1937–38. *CW*, vol. xiv.
> *The General Theory of Employment, Interest and Money*. 1936. *CW*, vol. vii.
> "How to Pay for the War." 1940. *CW*, vol. xxii.
> *Indian Currency and Finance*. London: Macmillan, 1913. *CW*, vol. i.
> *A Tract on Monetary Reform*. 1923. *CW*, vol. iv.
> *A Treatise on Money*. London: Macmillan, 1930. *CW*, vols. v & vi.
> *Treatise on Probability*. London, Macmillan, 1921. *CW*, vol. viii.

Keynes, John Maynard, with Hubert Henderson. "Can Lloyd George Do It? 1929. *CW*, vol. ix.

Leijonhufvud Axel. *Keynes and the Classics*. London: The Institute of Economic Affairs. 1969.

Moggridge D. E. *Maynard Keynes: An Economist's Biography*. London: Routledge, 1992.

Moore, G. E. *Principia Ethica*. Cambridge: Cambridge University Press, 1959.

O'Donnell R. M., ed. *Keynes as Philosopher-Economist*. London: Macmillan, 1991.

Patinkin, Don. *Keynes's Monetary Thought: A Study of Its Development*. Durham, NC: Duke University Press, 1976.

Schumpeter J. A. *Ten Great Economists*. London: Allen and Unwin, 1952.

Skidelsky Robert

John Maynard Keynes: Hopes Betrayed. London: Macmillan, 1983.

John Maynard Keynes: The Economist as Saviour. London: Macmillan, 1992.

John Maynard Keynes: Fighting for Britain. London: Macmillan, 2000.

John Maynard Keynes: Economist, Philosopher, Statesman. Abridged. London: Macmillan, 2002.

MARK SKOUSEN

Frank Knight and the Origin of the Chicago School of Economics

Frank Knight dominated the intellectual atmosphere . . . [he] seemed to most of us, to epitomize the spirit of the university.

—James M. Buchanan[1]

He was clearly the dominant intellectual influence upon economics students at Chicago in the 1930s.

—George Stigler[2]

George Stigler, James Buchanan, and, to a lesser extent, Milton Friedman—all Nobel Laureates linked to the Chicago School—laud Frank H. Knight (1885–1972) as one of three professors who greatly influenced them. The other two are Jacob Viner and Henry Simons.

When Knight died in 1972, the *Journal of Political Economy*, published by the University of Chicago, devoted several issues to him—a rare compliment. Knight's influence has been considered so dominant that some have knighted him "father" or "grandfather" of the Chicago School. Is such a representation accurate?

My basic thesis is that Frank Knight had, on net balance, a positive influence in defending and improving the neoclassical model of Adam Smith in an age when neoclassical economics came increasingly under attack by institutionalists (Veblen), social engineers (Pigou and Keynes), and Marxists. But in criticizing these critics, he had the annoying habit of adopting some of their arguments. It can be difficult to recognize Knight's positive contributions because they can be concealed by his rambling and obscure writings and his inconsistent and sometimes contradictory philosophy.

Knight's Personal History

Frank Knight, the first of eleven children of evangelical Midwesterners, was a skeptic all his life, though he often returned to religious subjects. He once said that if he could come back as anyone it would be Max Weber, the great German sociologist.[3] Knight's younger brother, Bruce, also an economist, tells the story that at services one day their parents had the children sign pledges promising to attend church for the rest of their lives. Returning home, Frank (then age 14 or 15) gathered his siblings behind the barn, built a fire, and said, "Burn these things because pledges and promises made under duress are not binding."[4]

He pursued his doctorate at Cornell, which resulted in his magnus opus *Risk, Uncertainty and Profit* (1921). For the rest of his career, Knight was a voluminous writer of essays that were compiled and published by students and colleagues. He taught courses on price theory, comparative economic systems, and history of economic thought (David Ricardo was his favorite whipping boy) at the University of Chicago, where he spent most of his career, from 1927 until his retirement in 1955. He remained in Chicago the rest of his life, with emeritus status. In 1941 he helped form the Committee on Social Thought, where Friedrich Hayek and T. S. Eliot taught in the 1950s. His tenure at Chicago matched the presidency of Robert Hutchins (1929–1951), where Knight repeatedly defended the use of the modern works rather than the classics by Hutchins and Mortimer Adler (The Great Books series).[5]

Knight was known to enjoy telling risqué stories, sherry in hand, and to have admired the gloomy poetry of Thomas Hardy. As a professor, he was terribly disorganized and, according to Rose Friedman, two-thirds of his students got nothing out of his classes.[6] He was often sarcastic, cynical, and blunt. One student demanded a refund after Knight made negative comments about religion and the Catholic church in his history of economic thought course.[7]

And his writings are famous for their complexity.

When Chicago graduate Larry Wimmer wrote about Knight's emeritus status in the 1960s, he did not paint the picture of a venerated man. "By the time I was in Chicago (1960–1965), Frank Knight was this small, bent-over old man who would shuffle into the economics department offices almost every day, and walk up the stairs. He never took the elevator, never looked up, and surely never spoke to the students. If someone hadn't told you who he was you might have been inclined to believe that it was another of Chicago's homeless trying to find a warm place. He always wore the same tattered coat. A number of us were disappointed that he was not asked to give a lecture or speak to the students. I was in one seminar in which he asked questions. It was the only time I heard him speak. I went to Chicago on a Frank Knight scholarship. I would have appreciated some contact, and today would make the effort. Back then we tended to wait upon faculty to make the moves and rarely did they do so among first or second year graduate students."[8]

How Much a Chicago Economist?

One wonders if the Chicago Nobelists are rewriting history. On the surface Frank Knight does not appear to be a "Chicago economist" in the standard way we view Chicago economics today. For example, Friedman and Stigler are famous for using the most advanced statistical methods to test rigorously their theories in micro- and macroeconomics. In 1957, Knight admitted, "Price theory on the traditional lines (filled in with empirical-quantitative content) is by far the most scientific of the disciplines dealing with motivated human behavior, and the most usable in guiding social action."[9] Yet he seldom engaged in empirical work! In fact, many of his references to data were unsubstantiated. According to Stigler, "he was extremely dogmatic in his empirical generalizations—all without a trace of proof."[10]

Chicago economists are often thought of as monetarists who apply the quantity theory of money to their analysis of the business cycle. That was Friedman's great contribution. In his long career, Frank Knight wrote only one article on the subject, in 1941, and there he only hints at what constitutes sound monetary policy. Even then he concludes, "The monetary system can never be made automatic."[11] Worse, he appears to support a fundamental Keynesian/socialist notion that there can be no inherent "self-regulating" governor in a free-enterprise system. States Knight: "Its equilibrium is vague and highly unstable. Its natural tendency is to oscillate over a fairly long period and a wide range, between limits which are rather indeterminate."[12] Friedman, of course, came to the opposite conclusion after doing his monetary studies: "It is now widely agreed that the Keynesian proposition is erroneous on the level of pure theory.... There always exists in principle a position of full employment equilibrium in a free market economy."[13]

Keynesian Economics: Pro and Con

Many Chicago students reported that Knight was an opponent of Keynesian economics in the postwar era. In his 1950 American Economic Association (AEA) presidential address, he debunked Keynes for having "succeeded in carrying economic thinking well back to the dark age."[14]

Paul Samuelson recalls a conversation with Knight at an AEA meeting in the early 1950s where Knight bluntly told a group, "If there's anything I can't stand it's a Keynesian and a believer in monopolistic competition." "What about believers in the use of mathematics in economic analysis, Frank," asked a colleague. "Can't stand it either," he replied firmly.[15]

Knight wrote a largely negative review of Keynes's *General Theory* in 1937, which Henry Hazlitt included in his *Critics of Keynesian Economics*.[16] According to Knight, Keynes's theory of unemployment was "unsubstantiated," adding that he "simply cannot take this new and revolutionary equilibrium theory seriously." And yet—Knight almost always adds the caveats "but," "on the other hand," and "up to a point" to his views—Knight ultimately endorsed one of Keynes's cures for depression and unemployment, that is, "inflation."[17] Knight wisely rejected the "favourite American recipe" of raising wages to revive spending,[18] yet he joined Henry Simons, Jacob Viner, and other Chicago economists in the 1930s to advocate deficit spending and an expansionary monetary policy to end the Depression.[19] This pre-Keynesian counter-classical approach may surprise many conservatives and libertarians, but it is one that Friedman himself endorses during extreme economic conditions. "Keynes had nothing to offer those of us who had sat at the feet of Simons, Mints, Knight, and Viner."[20]

The Liberal Market Order

James Buchanan says that he was "converted into a zealous advocate of the market order" when he took Knight's price theory course after the war in 1945. Buchanan notes that at the time almost every student, including himself, was a socialist.[21] Knight converted him. Surely that fits into the Chicago mold, which is famous for its market ideology. (I should add that Jacob Viner, who also taught price theory at Chicago, was pro-market. Friedman called Viner's price theory class "unquestionably the greatest intellectual experience of my life.")[22] Knight spent most of his career opposing the efforts of progressives, institutionalists, Keynesians, and Christians (he was known to make negative, sometimes insulting, comments about the Catholic church) who advocated social control in the name of science and morality. "I believe that individualism must be the political philosophy of intelligent and morally serious men.... It is my conviction that any great extension of state action in economics is incompatible with political liberty, that 'control' will call for more control and tend to run into complete regimentation...and finally into absolutism, with or without a destructive struggle for power."[23]

Yet here again Knight's philosophy was not always consistent. His price theory class was largely pro-market, and his overarching theme was favorable toward Adam Smith's "system of natural liberty," but he always insisted that the market system suffered from "imperfections," particularly two major flaws: a tendency toward monopoly power, and greater inequality of income and wealth. "On the other side, there is an undeniable natural tendency toward greater inequality and concentration of power under free enterprise itself, which political action seems the only way of counteracting."[24] His answer was antitrust and progressive and inheritance taxation.[25] His disciple and colleague Henry Simons advocated similar legislation.[26]

In the next generation at Chicago, Friedman and Stigler proved Knight and Simons wrong on both counts. Yet, at regular luncheons with Friedman and Stigler in the 1950s, Knight persisted in advocating these fundamental weaknesses in the free enterprise system. Stigler reports, "In later years at countless lunches this was challenged on both analytical and empirical grounds by Milton Friedman, each time leading Knight to make temporary concessions, only to return to his standard position by the next lunch."[27]

A Doubting Knight

During the 1930s, Knight lost faith in the "liberal market order" and fell into a deep pessimism from which he never fully recovered. He confessed, "For the first two years or so after the economic crisis of 1929, I was one of the large group of students of economics who condemned the idea that this was fundamentally different from other depressions. But I have become convinced that I was in error, that we are actually in the course of one of the world's great economic and political revolutions."[28] In an essay on "The Sickness of Liberal Society," written after two world wars and a Great Depression, Knight contended that the "free enterprise system of organization" (he preferred this term to the Marxist-inspired word "capitalism")[29] was full of "imperfections" and could not achieve a just and efficient society.[30] While at later times he denounced Marxism as "romantically immoralistic, destructive, diabolical," even "monstrous," and Marx as "a hater" of a "very high rank,"[31] he toyed with the idea of communism as an alternative social order in the early 1930s, at the depths of the Depression, when he gave a series of lectures under the provocative title "The Case for Communism: From the Standpoint of an Ex-Liberal." Rose and Milton Friedman attended one of these lectures, which they felt were "tongue-in-cheek" and aimed at attracting a large crowd. (Milton Friedman recalls that a majority of the students in the social sciences at Chicago at the time were members of the Communist Party or very close to it.) In a published version, Knight insisted that "liberalism, made up of economic laissez-faire and political democracy, is bankrupt." He confessed to contributing $20 to the socialist Norman Thomas and concluded, "What the nations of the world need today is government…a Communist Party dictatorship would be a real government; it would lead, unify and direct social activity and this is rapidly becoming essential to a tolerable existence."[32] Warren J. Samuels explains Knight's temptation with communism by explaining that "Knight was very much taken with freedom. But he was also a devotee of order," which communism provided.[33] Knight later regretted making these speeches: "I wish I could unpublished them."[34]

Yet into the 1960s he constantly preached a middle way between the extremes of Marxism and laissez-faire. "Marxist economics is a tissue of absurdity, but, sad to say, much nonsense has also been published by advocates of *laissez-faire*," he said. "Anarchism . . . is indefensible. . . . [S]ocial life sets many limits to freedom," he explained.[35]

An "Austrian" Economist?

In some ways, Knight can be viewed more an Austrian than a Chicago economist. He was fluent in German, and he corresponded with Hayek. We don't normally think of Knight as an Austrian because of his zestful attacks on the Austrian theory of capital (to be discussed below) and on Hayek's writings on political economy.[36] But there are some similarities. Kenneth Boulding noted that *Risk, Uncertainty and Profit* has a "distinctly 'Austrian' twist" to it, with its emphasis on entrepreneurship, imperfect competition, and decentralized decisionmaking.[37] Like Mises, he seldom used graphs or charts in his writings. His price theory textbook used in the 1930s has only two diagrams, and his chapter on supply and demand contains not a single supply-and-demand graph.[38] He distinguished between the social and natural sciences, and was naturally skeptical of applying mathematical constructs and quantitative analysis to economics. He often belittled the possibility of doing accurate empirical work: "It is not conceivably possible to 'verify' any proposition about 'economic' behavior by any 'empirical' procedure, if the key words of this statement are defined as they must be defined to be used with relevance and precision."[39]

Knight, like Mises and Hayek, offered incisive criticism of the theory of socialism, noting that central planners lack diverse knowledge (a Hayekian theme) and proper incentives to run an economy efficiently. He concludes, "Socialists grossly oversimplify the organization prob-lem . . ." and while central planners can run "routine operations of a stationary economy," they might have a challenge trying to deal with a "dynamic" change.[40]

In 1948, at a time when England was nationalizing industries and the United States was contemplating the same, Knight worried that government intervention into the economy would led to full-scale socialism: "But it is my conviction that any great extension of state action in economics is incompatible with political liberty, that 'control' will call for more control and tend to run into complete regimentation."[41] In 1950, Mises gave a speech along the same lines, titled "Middle-of-the-Road Policy Leads to Socialism."[42]

Most Austrian was his persistent pessimism—as opposed to the cheery optimism of Freidman and other Chicagoans in the postwar era. Like Mises and Hayek, Knight was not optimistic about the future of capitalism. In his 1950 AEA presidential address, he said he could "find little cause for jubilation," and bemoaned the lack of sound economic thinking by the public and government officials who favored protectionism, cheap money, tax evasion, and price-fixing. "The cards are heavily stacked in favor of centralization," he concluded.[43]

Knight as the Philosopher of Skepticism

Until now, we have largely focused on Frank Knight the critic, for which he was most famous. In fact, it was this critical eye that students found attractive. Knight was Buchanan's "role model." (Buchanan has only two photos on his wall—one of Frank Knight and the other of Swedish economist Knut Wicksell.) Why Knight? It was his "willingness to question anything, and anybody, on any subject anytime; the categorical refusal to accept anything as sacred; the genuine openness to all ideas, and, finally, the basic conviction that most ideas peddled about are nonsense or worse when examined critically."[44]

This became known as the Knightian trademark: committing economics (and other social sciences) to extremely rigorous and detailed examination, with numerous "ifs," "buts," "whens," "limitations," and the phrases "on the one hand," "on the other hand," and "up to a point." Knight opposed strict rules and formulas. He was the ultimate skeptic, always extremely cautious about the application of scientific methods. His nihilism went so far that he could state, "The only good principle is to have no principle."[45]

Friedman and Stigler picked up this Knightian trait of questioning
authority and constant criticism. Knight and his disciples looked upon
received theory, including the new theories of Keynes, with a highly
skeptical eye. "Frank Knight was a radical critic, who exhibited little
respect for the 'classical,' whether in Greek philosophy or in British
political economy."[46] He was disdainful of rank and authority. "Challenge everything," he said, that does not have logic or empirical support.
"There is no God, but Frank Knight is his prophet."[47]

The timing was right for this kind of skepticism. In an age when
nearly everyone on campus was a socialist or communist, Knight's
antiestablishmentarianism helped Buchanan become a libertarian.
Perhaps Knight had a similar effect on Friedman and Stigler, allowing
them to develop sufficient independence and irreverence of authority
to question the Keynesian monolith in the postwar era.

Given his dogmatic skepticism, a school of disciples was never
possible. (Schumpeter likewise never developed his own school.) Knight
did not fit into any particular research program. He was purely an ivory-
tower academic who did not consult with the government or the private
sector. According to Buchanan, "The world was not there waiting to be
'saved' by his own efforts, and he would have steadfastly refused to give
advice to a reforming despot.... His self-assigned task was to expose
the absurdities of others and nothing more."[48] He distrusted reformers:
"[P]eople have too much faith in positive action."[49]

Mistrust of Reformers

When it came to public policy, or "preaching," Stigler (though not
Friedman) would later follow Knight's path in maintaining a form of
agnosticism when it came to influencing legislators and politicians.
"My central thesis is that economists exert a minor and scarcely detect-
able influence on the societies in which they live."[50] Furthermore,
democratic institutions do a good job of reflecting voters' interests, and
therefore economists should beware of preaching or chastising them for
committing bad economic policy: "Economists...should be reluctant
to characterize a large fraction of political activity as mistaken."[51] The
political apathy of Stigler and Knight may explain the apolitical attitude
of graduate economics students at Chicago.

Knight the Sociologist

Perhaps we can think of Knight ultimately as a sociologist along the lines of the German sociologist Max Weber, who was trained as an economist. As Knight grew older, he showed less and less interest in pure economics and more and more interest in broader questions of law, ethics, philosophy, religion, anthropology, and political science. He taught courses on Max Weber at Chicago, and translated Weber's *General Economic History* into English in 1927. In 1941, he helped establish the Committee on Social Thought, an interdisciplinary program. In general, "Weber was more systematic, Knight an ad hoc sociologist," states Arthur Schweitzer.[52] Knight differed from Weber in methodology; Knight contended that economic laws are universal, Weber argued that laws must be verified with experience and claimed a "cultural science" of sociology based on time and place. One can see the influence of Weber in this statement by Knight on individualism and society: "The individual is largely formed in and by the social process, and the nature of the individual must be affected by any social action."[53]

Knight's Early Contributions
to Economic Science

Ultimately, Knight was a better critic than a systemic contributor of new theories. Nevertheless, he did make several important contributions to economic science, especially in countering the critics of the market.

His most famous work, *Risk, Uncertainty and Profit,* published in 1921, was used as a textbook at Chicago, Harvard, and the London School of Economics, and has been reprinted many times. (It is still in print, though not used as a textbook.) Several aspects of this classic work are worth noting.

Knight's book contains his chief contribution to the theory and nature of the role of profits in the competitive model. Essentially, he seeks to legitimatize the existence of profits in the market process and to defend it against critics who argued that profits were unjustified and unnecessary. Knight begins by defending theoretical (that is, deductive) economics with the use of "unrealistic" assumptions of "perfect competition." (Knight was the first to outline these basic assumptions.) Under the rigorous assumptions of perfect competition (many buyers and sellers, perfect knowledge, costless transportation, etc.), profit would be nonexistent. Entrepreneurs would move quickly from areas of lowest return to areas of highest return, and profit would disappear. How then can profit be justified?

By relaxing the assumption of perfect knowledge, the element of "uncertainty" becomes a part of the economic game, justifying profits. Here Knight makes a critical distinction between risk and uncertainty. Risk, he notes, is a measurable probability that can be insured against, such as life expectancy. But uncertainty is immeasurable, such as predicting short-term fluctuations in the stock market or foreign exchange rates, or even women's fashions.[54] Knight argued that the entrepreneur, especially in larger business enterprises, is compensated for bearing the uncertainties of the marketplace.

Critique of Pigou's Welfare Economics

Knight made a seminal criticism of Pigou's social welfare thesis, Keynesian interventionism, and socialist central planning. In an article titled "Some Fallacies in the Interpretation of Social Cost," published in 1924, he rejected Arthur C. Pigou's classic view of *The Economics of Welfare* (1920) that the laissez-faire market mechanism necessarily failed to achieve efficient allocation of resources. One example was road congestion. Suppose, he said, there are two roads connecting two cities. One road is cheap but badly surfaced, the other is narrow but well-graded (with more costly upkeep). Pigou concludes that the better road will be overused and overcrowded. The solution to this market failure would be to impose a tax equal to the difference between the average cost and marginal cost on the well-surfaced road.

Knight showed that if roads were privately owned, road owners would set tolls that would reduce congestion, and therefore no government tax would be required to establish an efficient use of resources.[55] On a broader scale, Knight's pioneering essay demonstrates that a free competitive environment can allocate resources efficiently as long as property rights are clearly identified. Knight's seminal article encouraged disciples, including Buchanan, Armen Alchian, and Ronald Coase, to study property rights and externalities.

Knight's Pedagogy: A Mix of Austrian and Chicago Economics

Knight came back to Chicago in 1927, and joined Viner in teaching the basic course in economic price, value, and distribution theory. The course is more fully developed in his textbook, *The Economic Organization* (1933), which made a major contribution to methodology.

Like his book, *Risk, Uncertainty and* Profit, Knight began his discussion of economic theory and the "economic man." He recognized the criticism of Veblen and others that economic man is not actually the social man of the world, and "does not include all human interests."[56] But, Knight argued, the theory of economic man, however one-dimensional, is a useful construct, consisting of a consumer maximizing utility and a producer maximizing profits, and therefore optimizing economic welfare and standard of living.

As mentioned earlier, Knight has only two diagrams in his text-book, one reflecting an Austrian view of the macroeconomy and the other representing the Chicago (and later Keynesian) view of the aggregate economy. On page 41 of his book, Knight illustrates the Austrian stages-of-production approach, showing how resources are transformed into final consumer and investment good, with examples of direct and indirect means to satisfying wants.

On page 61, Knight illustrates the "wheel of wealth" diagram, known today as the "circular flow" diagram. Today only Knight's "circular flow" diagram has been adopted by the profession, and with few exceptions the "stages of production" diagram has been omitted from the textbooks. This is due to Knight's decision in the 1930s to reject the stage-of-production model and Austrian theory of capital, which he regarded as unnecessary. His fatal decision has affected two disastrous effects on modern macroeconomics. First, by creating an excessively aggregate model of the economy, the circular-flow diagram has lead to several fallacies in macroeconomics. For example, it leads to the purchasing-power fallacy, that an increase in income through government spending or a minimum wage can stimulate output.

In addition, the Keynesians (Paul Samuelson, in particular) borrowed Knight's invention of the circular flow diagram to create the Keynesian "paradox-of-thrift" diagram, where savings can leak out of the economy and cause depression. In it we see that the key to economic stability and growth is consumer spending, which drives the circular flow of the economy, while savings leak out of the system.

The Austrians have pointed out that the Samuelson/Knight diagram ignores time and the production process. When the economy is driven by saving and investment, consumption (utility) is the effect, not the cause, of production.

It is a pity Knight didn't continue to preach the dynamic capital-using process of market activity.

Quantity Theory of Money

Knight's critique of the Austrian theory of capital reinforced Friedman's macroeconomics and his quantity theory of money. Knight's own view of capital and production was along the lines of John Bates Clark, who in an earlier era had attacked Böhm-Bawerk's period-of-production concept. Earlier in his career, Knight accepted the Austrian theory of capital: "I completely accepted it for years, taught it in class lectures and expounded it in text materials," including *The Economic Organization*.[57] But in the early 1930s, he abandoned the Austrian theory and echoed Clark's macro view: "In a stationary economy there is no interval between production and consumption."[58]

In 1934, he expounded a Fisherian version of capital and interest as a stock-flow concept, where capital is a permanent asset that yields future income, and criticized the flaws he saw in the time-structural view of a period of production. For Knight, like the circular flow diagram, "all capital is inherently perpetual."[59]

Throughout the early 1930s, Knight attacked Friedrich Hayek and his theory of business cycles, which was based on a Mengerian time structure of production and heterogeneous capital. Knight dismissed Hayek's theory as "worthless." In 1950, in an introduction to Carl Menger's newly translated *Principles of Investment*, Knight attacked one of Menger's fundamental principles of macroeconomics: "Perhaps the most serious defect in Menger's economic system...is his view of production as a process of converting goods of higher order into goods of lower order."[60]

If capital is indeed perpetual and homogeneous like putty, or water (Clark compared capital investment to the Hudson River), then a structural model is unimportant, and the Austrian theory of the business cycle is "useless."

Knight's dismissal of Austrian capital and business cycle theory was so strong that it influenced his students. In the 1950s, so the story goes, Knight would ask his students the following question on tests: "What do you know about Austrian capital theory?" The only acceptable answer was, "Nothing." According to Larry Wimmer, "Any more than that suggested a misallocation of their time and study. This is folklore; I have no idea if it actually happened."[61] Knight's dogma spread. Friedman and Stigler inherited this disdain for Austrian capital theory. (Stigler dismissed the Austrian theory of production and interest in his published dissertation.)[62] Knight's influence on Friedman is even more profound in this regard. Friedman's quantity theory of money is based entirely on a stock-flow model, where an increase in the money supply, like water, spreads evenly through the monetary river. (Friedman prefers to use the helicopter example for inflation.) Because capital investment is homogeneous, the transmission mechanism is simple and straightforward. Ripple effects are unimportant. What matters is that the height of the river rises.

Thus, the official Chicago view of monetary inflation is a simplistic monetary disequilibrium model, where changes in the money supply cause changes in economic activity. There is little concern over structural imbalances, asset bubbles, and interest-rate distortions. They are of secondary importance. The primary emphasis is on monetary trends, either "easy" or "tight" money as measured by the monetary aggregates. It all comes out of Knight.

Critique of Knight's Macro View

Other economists disagree, including Fritz Machlup and Israel Kirzner. Machlup called Hayek's capital theory an "indispensable" tool of analysis. "There was and is always the choice between maintaining, increasing, and consuming capital," he wrote in defense of Hayek.[63] Kirzner notes, "Because the Knightian view of the productive process emphasizes the repetitive 'circular flow' of economic activity while denying the paramount importance of a structural order linked to final consumer demand, it is possible to simply ignore the Austrian critique of the productivity theory of interest."[64]

The Austrian stages-of-production model is a more complex depiction of economic activity. It focuses on the importance of capital investment, interest rates, savings, and the right balance between production and consumption. It emphasizes the legitimacy of genuine natural savings as the key to economic performance, not increases in the money supply. It warns of asset bubbles and structural imbalances as a result of monetary intervention. It treats capital as heterogeneous, not just homogeneous. (Capital is liquid and homogeneous until it is invested in specialized capital goods.) It tells us more than the simplistic monetary disequilibrium model of Friedman and the monetarists.

There is a way to test which theory is best. What would be the effect of a steady 10 percent increase in the money supply? The Chicago School would say that this would cause inflation, a real rise in prices beyond the long-term growth rate of the economy. Say the economy is growing at 4 percent. Then inflation would be 6 percent, and would stay at around 6 percent as long as the central bank expanded the money supply steadily at a 10 percent rate. The Austrians would argue that there is an inherent law of diminishing returns at work here, that even with a steady annualized increase of the money supply by 10 percent, at some point the booming inflationary economy would collapse and head into recession or worse because inflation is "unsustainable."

Conclusion

I like to think of Frank Knight as the "knight" of the Chicago school, and I think he would be pleased with this designation. In the game of chess, the knight is not the most powerful piece on the board. Frank Knight is not the king or queen of the social sciences; that belongs to an Adam Smith, a Carl Menger, or a Milton Friedman. But he has a unique status. The knight is the most versatile of players: The horse jumps, can capture an enemy, and plays alternatively on white and black squares. He is the only piece that can move at the beginning of the game before any pawn move has been made. It is usually brought into play slightly sooner than the bishops (Frank Knight would like that), and much sooner than the king, queen, or rooks. To be most influential, the horse should be placed near the center of the board. A horse on the side or corner is ineffective. As chess players say, "A knight on the rim is grim."

Finally, the knight never plays it straight. The horse moves two squares forward and then moves to the left or right. He is a bit unpredictable. Frank Knight was always giving two cheers rather than three for the market.

George Stigler, who embodied much of the Knightian spirit, spoke the following at a 1972 memorial service: "Frank Knight transmitted, to a degree I have never seen equaled, a sense of unreserved commitment to the truth."[65] To which I add St. Paul's comment, "ever learning, and never able to come to the knowledge of the truth."[66]

Notes

[1] James M. Buchanan, "Frank H. Knight," *Remembering the University of Chicago*, ed. Edward Shils (Chicago: University of Chicago Press, 1991), p. 244.

[2] George Stigler, "Frank H. Knight," *The New Palgrave Dictionary of Economics* (London: Macmillan, 1987), 3: 56.

[3] Arthur Schweitzer, "Frank Knight's Social Economics," *History of Political Economy* 7 (3; 1975): 279.

[4] Stigler, "Frank H. Knight," *New Palgrave Dictionary*, 3: 55.

[5] See Ross B. Emmett, "Introduction," *Selected Essays by Frank H. Knight* (Chicago: University of Chicago Press, 1999), 1: xvii–xix.

[6] Rose Friedman: "We have often remarked that two-thirds of his students never got anything from him, and the rest never got anything out of two-thirds of his remarks, but that remaining one-third of one-third was well worth the price of admission. To this day we find ourselves often prefacing a comment, 'as Frank Knight would say.'" *Two Lucky People* (Chicago: University of Chicago Press, 1999), p. 38.

[7] Stigler comments, "Knight was both a great and an absurd teacher. The absurdity was documented by his utterly disorganized teaching, with constant change of subject

and yet insistent repetition of arguments...." *Lives of the Laureates*, 4th ed., ed. William Breit and Barry T. Hirsch (Cambridge, MA: MIT Press, 1998 [1986]), p. 81.

[8]Larry Wimmer (Brigham Young University) to Mark Skousen. Private correspondence, December 2005.

[9]Frank H. Knight, "Preface to the 1957 reprint," *Risk, Uncertainty and Profit* (New York: Harper & Row, 1921), p. lix.

[10]George J. Stigler, "Frank Hyneman Knight," *New Palgrave Dictionary*, 3: 56.

[11]Knight, "The Business Cycle, Interest and Money" in *Selected Essays*, 2: 146. Appeared originally in *The Review of Economics and Statistics* 23 (May 1941): 53–67.

[12]Ibid., p. 145.

[13]Milton Friedman and David Meiselman, "The Relative Stability of Monetary Velocity and the Investment Multiplier in the United States, 1897–1958," Commission on Money and Credit, *Stabilization Policies* (Englewood Cliffs, NJ: Prentice-Hall, 1963), p. 167.

[14]Frank H. Knight, "The Role of Principles in Economics and Politics" in *Selected Essays*, 2: 362–63.

[15]Paul A. Samuelson, *The Collected Scientific Papers of Paul A. Samuelson* (Cambridge: MIT Press, 1997), 4: 886-87.

[16]Henry Hazlitt, ed. *The Critics of Keynesian Economics* (Princeton, NJ: D. Van Nostrand. 1960).

[17]Knight, "Unemployment: And Mr. Keynes's Revolution in Economic Theory" in *Selected Essays*, 1: 345, 364–66.

[18]Frank H. Knight, "Social Science and the Political Trend," *Freedom and Reform* (Indianapolis: Liberty Fund, 1982 [1947]), pp. 26–27.

[19]J. Ronnie Davis, "Chicago Economists, Deficit Budgets, and the Early 1930's," *American Economic Review* 58 (June 1968): 477–78.

[20]Quoted in Robert J. Gordon, *Milton Friedman's Monetary Framework* (Chicago: University of Chicago Press, 1974), p. 163.

[21]James M. Buchanan, "Better than Ploughing," *Recollections of Eminent Economists*, ed. J. A. Kregel (New York: New York University Press, 1989), 2: 282.

[22]Interview in William Briet and Roger W. Spencer, eds., *Lives of the Laureates* (Cambridge: MIT Press, 1982), p. 83.

[23]Frank Knight, "Preface to the Reprint of 1948," *Risk, Uncertainty and Profit* (New York: Harper & Row, 1957 [1921]).

[24]Ibid., p. iii.

[25]Knight, "The Playful Act," *Freedom and Reform*, pp. 429–30, 451–53.

[26]Henry Simons, *Economic Policy for a Free Society* (Chicago: University of Chicago Press, 1948), pp. 57 passim.

[27]Stigler, "Knight," *New Palgrave Dictionary*, 3: 57.

[28]Knight, *Freedom and Reform*, pp. 27–28.

[29]Ibid., p. 448.

[30]Ibid., pp. 451–52.

³¹Knight, "Ethics and Economic Reform" in *Selected Essays*, 2: 34.

³²Frank H. Knight, "The Case for Communism: From the Standpoint of an Ex-Liberal," *Research in the History of Economic Thought and Methodology* (Greenwich, CT: JAI Press, 1991), Supplement 2: 53, 66, 92, 99, 106.

³³Warren J. Samuels, "Introduction," ibid., p. 52.

³⁴Quoted in Milton and Rose Friedman, *Two Lucky People* (Chicago: University of Chicago Press, 1998), p. 37.

³⁵Knight, "Laissez-Faire: Pro and Con," in *Selected Essays*, 2: 437.

³⁶Ibid., pp. 442–50. Knight heavily criticized Hayek's *Constitution of Liberty* (Chicago: University of Chicago Press, 1960), especially his treatment of economic equality, progressive taxation, and social justice.

³⁷Kenneth Boulding, jacket quote for Knight, *Risk, Uncertainty and Profit*.

³⁸Frank H. Knight, *The Economic Organization* (New York: Augustus M. Kelley, 1967 [1933]), pp. 67–95.

³⁹Knight, "What is Truth in Economics?" in *Selected Essays*, 1: 382.

⁴⁰Knight, "Socialism: The Nature of the Problem," in ibid., 2: 89, 95–96, 105. Originally published in *Ethics* 50 (April 1949).

⁴¹Knight, "Preface to 1948 Reprint," *Risk, Uncertainty and Profit*, p. iii.

⁴²Ludwig von Mises, *Planning for Freedom*, 4ᵗʰ ed. (Grove City, PA: Libertarian Press, 1980), pp. 18–35.

⁴³Knight, "The Role of Principles in Economics and Politics," in *Selected Essays*, 2: 361–62, 390.

⁴⁴Buchanan, "Better than Ploughing," *Recollections of Eminent Economists*, 2: 283.

⁴⁵Knight, *Selected Essays*, 1: ix.

⁴⁶Buchanan, "Frank H. Knight," *Remembering the University of Chicago*, p. 246.

⁴⁷Buchanan, Foreword, *Freedom and Reform*, xi.

⁴⁸Buchanan, "Frank H. Knight," in *Remembering the University of Chicago*, p. 251.

⁴⁹Frank H. Knight, "The Role of Principles in Economics and Politics" (his 1950 AEA presidential address) in *Selected Essays*, 2: 390.

⁵⁰George Stigler, *The Economist as Preacher, and Other Essays* (Chicago: University of Chicago Press, 1982), p. 63.

⁵¹Ibid., 8. Israel Kirzner wrote a scathing review of Stigler's essay on preaching, describing it as "bizarre…disturbing…unfortunate.…affront to common sense." See Kirzner in Daniel B. Klein, ed., *What Do Economists Contribute?* (New York: New York University Press, 1999), pp. 125–32.

⁵²Arthur Schweitzer, "Frank Knight's Social Economics," *History of Political Economy* 7 (3; 1975): 290.

⁵³Knight, *Freedom and Reform*, p. 69.

⁵⁴Knight, *Risk, Uncertainty, and Profit*, p. 233.

⁵⁵Frank H. Knight, "Some Fallacies in the Interpretation of Social Cost," *Quarterly Journal of Economics* 38 (May 1924): 582–606.

⁵⁶Frank H. Knight, *The Economic Organization* (New York: Augustus M. Kelley, 1967 [1933]), p. 4.

[57]Frank H. Knight, "Professor Hayek and the Theory of Investment," *Economic Journal* (March 1935): 79.

[58]Frank H. Knight, "Capitalistic Production, Time and the Rate of Return," *Economic Essays in Honour of Gustav Cassel* (London: George Allen and Unwin, 1933), p. 339.

[59]Frank H. Knight, "Capital, Time, and the Interest Rate," *Economica,* New Series 3 (August 1934): 264.

[60]Frank H. Knight, "Introduction," *Principles of Economics* (New York: New York University Press, 1959), p. 25.

[61]Larry Wimmer to Mark Skousen. Private correspondence, January 29, 2006.

[62]George Stigler, *Production and Distribution Theories* (New York: Macmillan, 1941). However, Rose Friedman did her own dissertation on capital theory under Professor Knight. It has been rumored that her dissertation, never finished, was sympathetic toward the Austrians. When I asked her about this recently, she nodded her head with a smile, but never said a word (perhaps because her husband Milton is staunchly critical of Austrian capital theory).

[63]Fritz Machlup, "Professor Knight and the 'Period of Production,'" *Journal of Political Economy* 43 (5; 1935): 578.

[64]Israel Kirzner, "Ludwig von Mises and the Theory of Capital and Interest," *Economics of Ludwig von Mises,* ed. Lawrence S. Moss (Kansas City: Sheed and Ward, 1976), p. 62.

[65]Quoted in Friedman, *Two Lucky People,* p. 36.

[66]2 Timothy 3:7.

LEE A. COPPOCK

James Buchanan:
Pioneer for Individual Freedom

Introduction

In 1986, James Buchanan was awarded the Nobel Prize in Economics. This was a vindication of him, of his ideas, and of his method of inquiry because James Buchanan has never been an academic insider. He received his bachelor's degree from Middle Tennessee State Teacher's College; his academic appointments include Chico State in California.

When asked about his status as an academic outsider, Buchanan often stresses that it is important to him because it has enabled him to explore ideas in an almost unconstrained fashion. He has never felt the need to have his ideas conform to some ideal held by a department in which he might reside.

In examining Professor Buchanan's contributions to economics, I will, of course, emphasize his work in Public Choice economics. But I would be remiss if I skipped over his work in other areas. To encompass the variety of his efforts, I will follow a chronology of his accomplishments.

Chicago

Frank Knight of the University of Chicago, a founder of the Chicago School, was an inspiration, a role model, and a methodological father to James Buchanan. He ascribes to Knight the credit for his continued determination to question everything, to take nothing as sacred in the development of ideas.

When Buchanan arrived in Chicago, he was a self-described "libertarian-socialist." Apparently he had conflicting ideas swimming in his head. As a Southerner, he had an unquestionable distrust of federal government. But he also had a very real mistrust and dislike of large corporations, banks, and inherited money. After six weeks of Frank Knight's classes, however, Buchanan left all of his socialist tendencies behind and embraced the principles of individual liberty—for good.

The other major influence on Buchanan during his days in Chicago was Knut Wicksell, whom he discovered by accident After he passed his German language exams, Buchanan went to the University of Chicago library where he stumbled onto a copy of Wicksell's works, which were written in German. He was absolutely enveloped by Wicksell's ideas. What he saw in Wicksell was the embodiment of much of what he himself had been thinking, but in a logical and written form. Much of Buchanan's work in *The Calculus of Consent* would be based on Wicksell.

Buchanan left Chicago a very competent neoclassical micro-economist with a distinct appreciation for individual liberty—and a determination to question everything. To see how this translated into his research, we will briefly examine two significant contributions Buchanan made in the 1960s that are not specifically Public Choice.

The first is a paper titled "Externality," which was published in 1962. This was Buchanan's attempt to formally address the issues raised by what economists call "externalities," which are one of the classic "market failures" that economists use to justify government intervention in the private marketplace. Externalities occur when some unrelated third party is affected by the behavior of a firm or individual. Economists in the 1960s (and some still today) would assume that the very appearance of an externality is evidence that the market has failed, and that government solutions must be forthcoming.

The classic externality problems are typically presented as negative production externalities. For example, Alsons Corporation, a firm located in Hillsdale, Michigan, produces showerheads. Suppose that in the production of their quality handheld showerheads, Alsons also produces something undesirable—noise. This noise is a negative externality imposed upon the company's neighbors, which include a number of farms.

Let's assume that showerhead production is very profitable and that there is a law against noise pollution. Suppose Alsons' production is so profitable the company can afford to both produce high quality showerheads *and* compensate the farmers for any damages. In other words, Alsons can pay the farmers for enduring the noise pollution and still make profit. In this world, the farmers are no worse off than they were previously and yet we still observe noise pollution. This scenario is not altogether unlikely.

Here is Buchanan's point: "There is not a prima facie case for intervention in all cases where an externality is observed to exist. The internal benefits from carrying out the activity, net of costs, may be greater than the external damage that is imposed on other parties."[1] Of course, his colleague at the University of Virginia, Ronald Coase, would do even more damage to the traditional externality position.

In a paper titled "An Economic Theory of Clubs," published in 1965, Buchanan goes after the second major "market failure." Following Paul Samuelson's paper (1954),[2] it was assumed throughout the economics profession that a public good was simply a requirement for government provision. In addition, the definition of a public good was much fuzzier in 1965. The fundamental characteristic of a Samuelsonian public good was merely "non-rivalry in consumption."[3] This means simply that the good in question can be simultaneously consumed by more than one individual without affecting the consumption (in quantity or quality) of another individual. An example of a public good is something like a levee: It protects several homes as well as it protects a single home. In contrast, an ice cream cone is a private good: Its consumption by one person absolutely affects the consumption by another.

Samuelson's paper essentially opened the door to significant government intervention. The reason is that there really are scores of goods that are, at least to some degree, nonrivalrous in nature. For example, a lecture has a degree of nonrivalry. You could add a few more students to the audience and there would be no real effect on the quality of the lecture that each individual hears. This applies to movies, golf, education, and many other things. In other words, if nonrivalry requires government provision, the role of government would be significant.

Buchanan's point here is simple: Many of these goods are provided (and provided well) privately. Often, these goods are provided in the form of a club. In fact, *as long as exclusion is feasible,* nonrivalrous goods can and will be provided efficiently by private markets. Buchanan's paper was significant in that it shifted the public goods debate to the characteristic of feasibility of exclusion.

Without his contributions to Public Choice economics, Professor Buchanan would certainly be viewed as a fine neoclassical economist and a champion of freedom. However, what earned him a Nobel Prize and what truly set him apart as a great economist was his path-breaking work in Public Choice theory. We turn to that work now, in reference to the seminal book published in 1962, co-written with Gordon Tullock, *The Calculus of Consent.*[4]

The Calculus of Consent

The basic approach of *The Calculus* stems directly from the work of Knut Wicksell and James Madison (a Virginian). From Wicksell, Buchanan takes the admonition that "economists have got to stop acting as if they are advising benevolent despots."[5] From Madison, he incorporates the skepticism of behavior and motives of politicians that are embodied in the U.S. Constitution and *Federalist Papers.* The basic approach of *The Calculus,* which many take to also be the thrust of Public Choice economics, is that actors in political markets are motivated by the same factors that influence the behavior of actors in private markets.

Economic behavior is rational utility-maximizing selfish behavior. Using this model of individual behavior, economists can explain much of what people do privately, both in their household and in their business firms. However, in the 1960s, economists (and even political scientists) studying government and political markets assumed a different type of behavior on the part of politicians and bureaucrats. The assumption was that individuals acting in political markets (voters, legislators, bureaucrats) act on behalf of their fellow man. However, individuals buying groceries or seeking education for their children or running a business can only be trusted to act out of selfish ambition. This means that one day someone could become the CEO of GM who is a greedy self-serving individual. However, if this person enters the voting booth, or is elected to office, or is nominated to serve as a bureaucrat, that person undergoes an instant transformation into a "public servant."

The Calculus uses the language and tools of neoclassical economics to formalize Madisonian insights. This adaptation of Madison to economics is what spawned the discipline that we call "Public Choice Economics." It is what earned Buchanan a Nobel Prize. It seems simple now, and perhaps it is, but at the time, it was nothing short of revolutionary.

When Buchanan recounts the intellectual environment of the 1960s in both the academy and the discipline of economics, he does so with near bewilderment. He can talk about how he and his colleagues— including fellow Nobel Prize winner Ronald Coase—were outcasts both in the discipline of economics and at their own university, the University of Virginia, which we still fondly refer to as Mr. Jefferson's university (isn't that ironic?). Many of their pioneering papers were published in second-tier journals.

In the field of economics, which was dominated by central-planning and the general thought that government can (and will) fix all the problems in the economy, Buchanan and Tullock basically exclaimed that "the emperor has no clothes, and he wants yours."

Here is the fundamental insight of *The Calculus* that led to a field of research: Government officials are just like you and me. They are interested in themselves, and they will use the resources at their disposal to enrich themselves and secure power. What does this mean for economic policy? It means that simple government solutions to market failures may prove worse than the problem.

The focus in the early part of *The Calculus* is on voting rules for collective decisions. There are two rules in particular that are viewed as benchmarks: simple majority and unanimity (which comes straight from Wicksell). What is so special about simple majority? Why is it that we often default to simple majority when making collective decisions? What is so special about fifty percent plus one? If we base collective activity (government action) on simple majority, then it only takes a simple majority to coerce the rest of the populace.

Buchanan and Tullock examine the costs of different voting rules. Imagine a continuum from 1 to 300. Along this continuum, we are measuring the number required to agree on an issue before collective action is taken. Call this the "necessary number." The rule of simple majority implies a necessary number of 151; the rule of unanimity requires a necessary number of 300.

At one extreme, when the necessary number is unity, collective action can be demanded when only one person votes in favor of it. At this extreme, *any* single person can make decisions on behalf of the group, and thus having the ability to require the group to act in certain ways. This sounds great if that person is me. But any person can do this. This is clearly a silly arrangement that would not last long in any society. At the other extreme, collective activity cannot be required without full consent of everyone in the population (unanimity). Somewhere in the middle of these extremes is simple majority (fifty percent plus one vote).

In order to search for an optimal necessary number on any particular issue, Buchanan and Tullock delineate two types of costs associated with changes in the necessary number. (The term "necessary number" is my own concoction. They probably wouldn't like it— too wordy.) That is, they distinguish two types of costs associated with increasing the size of the majority needed to undertake collective activity.

Buchanan and Tullock call the first decisionmaking costs. These rise with the necessary number. If the necessary number is one, these costs are zero, since no time or resources are expended in order to reach a decision. A single voter decides. However, as the necessary number increases toward 300, decisionmaking costs rise, and they rise more quickly as you approach 300. In fact, the costs of securing the very last vote can approach infinity, depending upon the issue, as the last voter realizes his bargaining position. That decisionmaking costs rise with the necessary number is why the rule of unanimity is infeasible for everyday collective activity decisions, such as referenda or decisions in the legislature. But don't worry—Buchanan finds a nice use for the rule of unanimity later.

A key contribution of *The Calculus* was to recognize a second type of cost from collective activity. In ironic fashion, the authors borrowed the classic "market failure" of externality. Because when activity is undertaken on behalf of the group, which by definition means that all must conform, this has the potential to force some into an activity of which they do not approve. For example, the collective activity could be a vote on the provision of a public good, such as a bridge. If a group of 300 has a simple majority rule, and 151 people decide that to fund the bridge redheads must pay a 75 percent marginal tax rate, people with red hair are out of luck. The majority can impose an external cost on redheads, even though no redheads voted for this proposal. There are external costs associated with private *and* public behavior.

But external costs decline as the necessary number rises. If only one person is needed for collective activity, then considerable external costs can be imposed on the rest of the population. However, if unanimity is required—that is, everyone must agree before collective activity is undertaken—then there will be no external costs imposed upon any voter. This is the beauty of the rule of unanimity: All must agree, so by definition, no external costs can be imposed. This is why Wicksell was so enchanted with the concept. If not for the decisionmaking costs, the rule of unanimity would dominate as a rule for collective activity.

Here are two practical applications of this analysis. Recognition of external costs seriously undermines the rule of simple majority. What is so special about this rule? Why is it that tax packages can be imposed upon the entire population with the agreement of only fifty percent plus one? Why is it that a 51 percent majority can require behavior from a 49 percent minority? A society that respects individual liberty should examine this rule carefully.

It is in a second practical application of this analysis that Buchanan finds a home for the rule of unanimity. That is the application to constitutional formation. When Buchanan talks about constitutions, he is simply referring to the rules of the game. These rules are important. In fact, in the years after the publication of *The Calculus*, Buchanan turned his attention to Constitutional Political Economy. Writing a constitution is essentially setting up the rules before the game begins. We do not know how the game will play out and so we do not know, *ex ante*, whether a particular rule will help us or harm us. We all may agree on a rule behind the Rawlsian "veil of ignorance." Here, in the formation of constitutions, Buchanan sees a very real role for the Wicksellian rule of unanimity.

Limits of Liberty

Moving beyond *The Calculus of Consent*, Buchanan's writings continued to be shaped by what was occurring in the world around him. The events of the 1960s took their toll on Professor Buchanan and they certainly affected his view of the world. He admits that *The Calculus* was written in a period of optimism, in the early 1960s, "as though he was looking at the world through rose-colored glasses." But he cites the turmoil on college campuses, the "purchase of the Presidency," and the Vietnam War as factors that changed his faith in the stability of democracy.

This change is reflected in a little book published in 1975 called *The Limits of Liberty*.[6] In it, Buchanan felt obligated to make the case for collective activity even if anarchy reigned. His starting point is no longer a stable democracy, but a Hobbesian jungle.

Buchanan uses a simple prisoner's dilemma analysis to justify coming together for collective action. Imagine an island with only two occupants and, initially, no laws: Anarchy reigns. On this island the two inhabitants grow their own food and spend most of their time cultivating the land. But they also have an incentive to steal from the land of the other. Both of them do. The incentives are such that if either one farms a little and steals a little, the outcome is easily the best case scenario for that one individual. That is, as long as the other inhabitant is farming exclusively. But since they both face the same incentives, they know that the best they can do is to farm a little and steal a little.

The problem is that if they both farm-and-steal, their society devolves and the outcome is certainly the least desirable for the island. Resources will also be spent on crop protection (staying up all night to guard, building fences). In this world, the equilibrium outcome (without any sort of collective action) is one in which they are both farming and stealing and guarding. This is not an optimal outcome for either of the two island inhabitants. But neither one has the incentive to just farm.

Here is the impetus for collective action, for group agreement. It would be in the interest of both farmers to adopt a constitution that reads: "Any inhabitant caught stealing will lose a finger." They can even come to unanimous agreement on this (as it occurs at the constitutional stage). What this constitution allows them to do is to reach the best possible scenario in which they both spend all their time producing. Thus, the incentives for collective activity arise even in a world where evil pervades and no legal structure exists initially.

Conclusion

When most people think about Public Choice economics, they cite the many papers built on the insight of *The Calculus of Consent*: the insight that individuals acting in political markets are motivated by the same factors that motivate people in private markets. But for Buchanan, this contribution is not enough. For him, it leaves a void with regard to economic theories of politics. But in fact, there is something positive that economic analysis can add to political theory. This contribution is that voluntary collective action can take place and through voluntary exchange, it is possible to help each member of a polity.

Buchanan cites Madison's *Federalist* 12. In this paper, Madison argues that it will be to the benefit of all states in the union to form a federal government: It will be easier to protect as the numbers of exposed borders shrinks to one. In the same way, Buchanan believes, individuals can come together for voluntary exchange and so form a collective entity and agree on a constitution that can benefit all.

Notes

[1]James M. Buchanan and W. Craig Stubblebine,"Externality," *Economica* 29 (116; 1962): 371–84, esp. p. 381.

[2]Paul Samuelson, "The Pure Theory of Public Expenditure," *Review of Economics and Statistics* (November 1954): 387–89.

[3]James M. Buchanan, "An Economic Theory of Clubs," *Economica*, 32 (125; 1965): 1–14.

[4]James M. Buchanan and Gordon Tullock, *The Calculus of Consent* (Ann Arbor: University of Michigan Press, 1965).

[5]See http://oll.libertyfund.org/Home3/Audio.php?recordID=0517.23. The podcast is © 2005 The Liberty Fund.

[6]James Buchanan, *The Limits of Liberty: Between Anarchy and Leviathan* (Chicago: University of Chicago Press, 1975).

Robert J. Barro

Milton Friedman: General Perspectives and Personal Reminiscences

When my son Jason was an economics Ph.D. student at Harvard in the 1990s, he said: "I have observed that only two economists can push you around, Milton Friedman and Gary Becker." I agreed, but argued that it was a good thing. Everyone needs heroes, and Gary had only Milton. Milton had no one, except Ronald Reagan in the 1980s, but Reagan does not qualify as an economist. Arthur Burns may once have been the economist hero—as an instructor at Rutgers, he apparently helped to persuade the undergraduate Milton not to be an actuary. However, Burns's exalted status ended in 1971 when he went over to the dark side by endorsing Richard Nixon's outrageous price controls. Milton tells me that Frank Knight was also his "god," presumably between 1932 and 1935 when Milton was a graduate student at the University of Chicago and after 1946, when Milton joined the Chicago faculty.

His long-time friend George Stigler told the story of how Milton got his faculty appointment at Chicago. The two were together in 1945–46 on the faculty of the University of Minnesota. In his *Memoirs of an Unregulated Economist*, Stigler says:

> In the spring of 1946 I received the offer of a professorship from the University of Chicago, and of course was delighted at the prospect. The offer was contingent upon approval by the central administration after a personal interview. I went to Chicago, met with the President, Ernest Colwell, because Chancellor Robert Hutchins was ill that day, and I

was vetoed! I was too empirical, Colwell said, and no doubt that day I was. So the professorship was offered to Milton Friedman, and President Colwell and I had launched the new Chicago School. We both deserve credit for that appointment, although for a long time I was not inclined to share it with Colwell.[1]

It was not until 1958 that Stigler left Columbia to accept the lucrative Walgreen Professorship and was then reunited with Milton in Chicago.

The only person to rival Milton for policy influence in the twentieth century was John Maynard Keynes, who had a strikingly different view of the role of government. Keynes advocated more government intervention into what he perceived as poorly functioning private economies caught up in the global depression of the 1930s. In contrast, Milton put the primary blame for the U.S. depression on government failure, especially of the Federal Reserve's monetary policy. Hence, the existence of the Great Depression posed no dilemma for Milton's broad preference for small government, and he found in the Fed's failures to prevent deflation an argument in favor of monetary rules. As the world evolved—with price stability becoming the major mission of central banks and free markets and property rights becoming the key policies to promote economic growth—Milton surely won the intellectual and policy battles.

Being held in high esteem by the economics profession was not always Milton's status, and he had to endure a long march from pariah to priest. This transition culminated in the Nobel Prize in Economics in 1976, a great choice that confirmed the widespread impact of his economic ideas. In contrast, in the mid-1960s, when I started as a graduate student in economics at Harvard, my professors viewed Milton as a right-wing, Midwestern crank. Surprisingly, Milton was most notorious for his work on money, especially for the dictum that "inflation is always and everywhere a monetary phenomenon."[2]

Milton laid out his views on money in "The Quantity of Money— A Restatement" (an essay in the 1956 book, *Studies in the Quantity Theory of Money*) and the epic *A Monetary History of the United States* (written in 1963 with Anna Schwartz).[3] The *Monetary History* explores money-supply determination under different regimes, including the gold standard. Friedman and Schwartz argued that much of the historical variation in money supply was independent of shifts in the demand for money. They used this pattern to argue that the positive association between nominal money and real economic activity reflected primarily causation from money to the real economy, rather than the reverse.

My Harvard teachers argued that even Milton's permanent income theory of consumption, developed in his 1957 book, *A Theory of the Consumption Function*,[4] was flawed. In truth, Milton had constructed a scientifically impeccable model in which consumer demand depended on households' anticipated long-run income. The permanent-income idea is now a core component of all serious economic analyses of consumer behavior.

The odd thing from a current perspective is that Milton's stress on monetary disturbances was viewed in the 1960s as anti-Keynesian. It is true that Keynes in his *General Theory* deemphasized monetary disturbances as a source of business fluctuations, and he was also skeptical about the role of monetary policy as an anti-recession device. However, particularly since the 1980s, self-styled New Keynesians have embraced activist monetary policy as a centerpiece of counter-cyclical policy. Thus, Milton's stress on the business-cycle effects of monetary shocks now fits comfortably—maybe too comfortably—with Keynesian thinking.

Milton refined his views on money in his 1967 presidential address to the American Economic Association (AEA). "The Role of Monetary Policy," which appeared in the 1968 *American Economic Review*, is probably the most important contribution ever to come from this format. Usually presidential addresses and similar speeches cannot be forgotten too soon. A key result—which, along with work by Edmund Phelps, foreshadowed the 1970s Bob Lucas-led revolution on rational expectations macroeconomics—was that only unanticipated movements in money and the price level mattered for real economic activity. However, Milton's monetary framework implied a potentially important role for activist monetary policy in smoothing out the business cycle. Systematic monetary changes had substantial short-term real effects, and wise interventions could improve the functioning of the macroeconomy. Implicitly, the private market was working badly, beset by sticky prices and wages in the short run, and the monetary authority could help by stimulating the economy in recessions and cooling things down in booms. No wonder that this part of Milton's monetary ideas would be embraced by Keynesians in the 1980s.

To go from Milton's monetary framework to an argument for monetary stability, one needs additional features, such as the "long and variable lags" stressed in *A Program for Monetary Stability*.[5] Even more important is the distinction between rules and authorities emphasized by Henry Simons (and subsequently analyzed in a large literature on rules versus discretion). Models with these features can explain why monetary activism often causes more harm than good, even when (or, rather, especially if) monetary shocks have major real effects. Thus, these extensions can reconcile Milton's conceptual framework with the constant-growth-rate rules for monetary aggregates that he favored in practical policy advice.

Milton has been very successful with the broad proposition that monetary policy activism tends to be mistaken. However, his well-known, specific proposal—that a monetary aggregate such as M1 or M2 grow at a prespecified rate such as 2 or 3 percent per year—has problems. In fact, this area is the only one I know of where Milton pretty much reversed his previous position. The problem is that the real demand for money is not that stable, most dramatically in the current, high-tech financial environment, but also over the longer history. Therefore, a constant growth rate for any monetary aggregate does not ensure anything close to inflation stability. One way or another, a monetary policy aimed at inflation stability has to allow the nominal quantity of money to adjust to shifts in the real quantity of money demanded. In modern inflation targeting, this accommodation works through changes in nominal interest rates, which respond to deviations of inflation (or, possibly, expected inflation) from target. As part of this process, nominal money adjusts automatically to shifts in real money demand. (In technical jargon, the nominal quantity of money is endogenous.)

Although these refinements of constant-growth-rate rules are important, the spirit of inflation targeting fits with Milton's general approach to monetary policy. Central banks ought not to be business-cycle doctors; if they can achieve inflation stability, they have more than done their jobs. In fact, and much to my surprise, central banks in most advanced economies have been remarkably successful since the late 1980s in attaining low and stable inflation. Moreover, instead of adverse consequences for output and employment, real performance has probably improved.

Despite his fame in the macroeconomic area, Milton's most important contributions to the policy debate are on the microeconomic side. His over-arching theme is the benefits from free markets and private enterprise. The conceptual framework is in the outstanding 1953 book, *Essays in Positive Economics*.[6] Many of the policy proposals were expressed as early as the 1950s and appeared in *Capitalism and Freedom*. This 1962 book, developed from a series of lectures in 1956, is the classic work on economic ideas for a general audience. I learn something every time I read this remarkable work, and who can forget the opening lines:

> In a much quoted passage in his inaugural address, President Kennedy said, "Ask not what your country can do for you—ask what you can do for your country." ... Neither half of the statement expresses a relation between the citizen and his government that is worthy of the ideals of free men in a free society. The paternalistic "what your country can do for you" implies that government is the patron, the citizen the ward, a view that is at odds with the free man's belief in his own responsibility for his own destiny. The organismic "what you can do for you country" implies that government is the master or the deity, the citizen, the servant or the votary. To the free man, the country is the collection of individuals who compose it, not something over and above them. He is proud of a common heritage and loyal to common traditions. But he regards government as a means, an instrumentality, neither a grantor of favors and gifts, nor a master or god to be blindly worshipped and served. He recognizes no national goal except as it is the consensus of the goals that the citizens severally serve. He recognizes no national purpose except as it is the consensus of the purposes for which the citizens severally strive.[7]

Capitalism and Freedom expressed numerous ideas once thought to be radical but now viewed as mainstream. The all-volunteer army has worked well in the United States and other countries for many years, privatized social security lives in Chile and other places, the U.S. earned-income tax credit is a form of negative income tax, the flat-rate income tax prevails in many countries (even Russia), school vouchers work in some U.S. localities and are under active consideration in others, and market-oriented welfare reform was enacted by Bill Clinton of all people. In addition, open capital markets are the norm in the developed world, and flexible exchange rates prevail in many countries. The spirit of monetary stability has also been accepted, though in the more modern form of inflation targeting. Some years from now we may add Milton's recent proposals on the decriminalization of drugs to the list of generally accepted proposals.

Anyone who wants to understand Milton's policy ideas should start with *Capitalism and Freedom* and then go to *Free to Choose*, the bestselling 1980 book from the television show that made Milton a household name. He notes in his autobiography—*Two Lucky People: Memoirs*, written in 1998 with his wife Rose—that France was the only European country never to air the television program.[8] Seems that some things never change. As evidence of the celebrity status conveyed by *Free to Choose*, I recall being on a trip with Milton when, in Chicago's O'Hare Airport, a man noticed my companion. The man was literally beside himself, in the manner of an avid fan coming in contact with a rock star.

I learned from *Memoirs* that Milton's influence was achieved mainly through the force of ideas, not by direct participation in the policy process. Except for work in 1935–1937 in New Deal Washington (when Milton had no academic job opportunities) and during World War II, Milton avoided government service. His key advice to academic economists: "by all means spend a few years in Washington—but only a few. If you stay more than two or three years you will become addicted and will be unable effectively to return to a scholarly career."[9] My only disagreement is that two or three years in Washington are too many.

In any event, Milton probably would not have been an outstanding policymaker. His main output in Washington during World War II involved work on the establishment of income-tax withholding. It may be that no other law has done more to enlarge the size of the federal government. Certainly Milton regrets the existence of income-tax withholding, but he also says (no doubt correctly) that this institution would be present even if he had never set foot in Washington.

Milton's *Memoirs* contain interesting views on the value of testifying before Congress and of writing popular commentaries. He says: "I long ago decided it was a waste of time to testify before Congressional committees. Spending the same time writing an op-ed piece or giving a talk is a more efficient use of time for the purpose of influencing policy."[10] I always remember Milton's opinion when I receive an invitation to testify before Congress, and I inevitably decline. I am also pleased that Milton regards commentary in popular media as potentially valuable, since I have spent a fair bit of time writing for *The Wall Street Journal* and *Business Week*. Milton's well-reasoned and lively writings in *Newsweek* from 1966 to 1984 are the model toward which any economic commentator ought to aspire. In *Memoirs*, he describes his initial nervousness about being able to generate enough topics to fill the columns. Hence, he did not accept *Newsweek's* offer until he had assembled a substantial list of potential ideas. But Milton says he never used anything from the list—something interesting and timely always came up, and he had no problem producing a column every three weeks.

Memoirs also verifies a well-known story about Milton's concern, as 1967 AEA president, about the association's accumulation of a substantial surplus. He worried that the money would be spent on some ill-advised project designed by a social do-gooder. Therefore, he successfully proposed the startup of a new journal (the *Journal of Economic Literature*) without increasing membership dues. The resulting budget deficit used up the endowment in a reasonably quick and nearly harmless manner. I remembered this episode when I was AEA vice president in 1998. Again, the association had accumulated a large surplus, and I worried about possible ill-advised uses. My proposal at the time (when the AEA already had three journals) was to cut the membership dues until the endowment declined to a reasonable level. However, lacking Milton's talents at persuasion, I failed miserably in this proposal. The problem of the large surplus was not solved until the stock market declined at the end of the Internet boom in 2000.

Milton is often cited, starting with *Time* magazine in December 1965, for the famous quote: "We are all Keynesians now." However, we learn from *Memoirs* that the quote was taken out of context to change the meaning. The full statement reconstructed by Milton in a letter to *Time* in 1966 is: "In one sense we are all Keynesians now; in another, nobody is any longer a Keynesian."[11] Milton explains that the first sense refers to the rhetoric and style of macroeconomic analysis—Keynes essentially invented macroeconomics as a distinct field. The second sense applies to substantive implications; specifically, to the idea that (almost) no one now advocates the simplistic policy activism recommended in Keynes's *General Theory*. Although the second observation is more significant, the first got the most press.

Milton also mentions a Keynes quote attributed in the 1960s to Richard Nixon: "Now I am a Keynesian in economics." This quote may help to explain the awful economic policies that Nixon carried out as president. Aside from price controls, his administration featured a sharp rise in federal spending, especially for Social Security, a large increase in inflation, the Endangered Species Act, the establishment of the Environmental Protection Agency, and the 55-mile-per-hour speed limit. A misery index based on inflation, unemployment, real GDP growth, and nominal interest rates reveals that Jimmy Carter was the only president with worse outcomes in the post-World War II period. As I have argued elsewhere, Nixon surely deserved to be impeached, but more for economic policy than for Watergate.

I cannot resist noting some intriguing personal linkages between Milton and me. First, we both have Hungarian origins, our families both came from territory that is now part of Ukraine. (My mother was from Munkacs, now Mukacevo; Milton's parents were from Beregszasz or Berehovo.) Second, I have the name Friedmann in my ancestry, though from my father's origins in Transylvania. Finally, in 1982, at the start of my second faculty position at the University of Chicago, I purchased the house at 5731 South Kenwood Avenue that the Friedmans had occupied from 1950 to 1962. (Milton once asked me about the fine workbench in the basement, and I told him that it was still there in 1984.)

Despite all these linkages, I regret that Milton's personal advice to me has not always been of the same quality as his policy advice. For instance, when I was Milton's colleague in 1974, I received an invitation to attend the Hong Kong meeting of the libertarian Mont Pèlerin Society. Since Milton was a founding member of the Society, I naturally solicited his opinion about whether I should attend. He replied that the Society ought to be abolished. Following the lines of a speech he gave at the 1972 meeting, he said that the Mont Pèlerin Society came into being after World War II to serve the needs of persons in countries where dialogues with fellow libertarians were impossible. The Society was highly successful in meeting this need through the 1960s. However, with the development of alternative institutions and the spread of global communications, Milton argued that this function was no longer necessary by the early 1970s. More generally, Milton thought that institutions have a tendency to live on or expand long after their missions were accomplished. Thus, he suggested that the Mont Pèlerin Society declare victory and go out of business, thereby setting a great example for other organizations that ought to fade away. My candidate list—which I think Milton would endorse—includes the International Monetary Fund, the World Bank, and the United Nations.

The problem with Milton's cogent analysis of the Mont Pèlerin Society and institutions more broadly is that I took it as personal advice not to attend the 1974 meeting. Therefore, I turned down the invitation. This was a mistake because I missed out on numerous exciting meetings of the Society until I first attended in 1992 in Vancouver.

In a similar vein, Milton advised me in 1973 to relinquish the tenured position I had at Brown University to accept a nontenured post at the University of Chicago. (I was a visitor at Chicago in 1972.) This advice reflected Milton's general antipathy toward the tenure system, some of which seems to derive from bad personal experiences in 1940–1941 with incompetent and hostile senior colleagues at the University of Wisconsin. Basically, Milton viewed tenure as a mechanism to ensure low work effort by many senior professors. (Milton did not explain, however, why tenure was an equilibrium outcome in the higher education market.)

Even if Milton was correct about the inefficiency of tenure as an institution, it was a fallacy of composition to conclude that tenure was unimportant for me individually. But, not making this connection, I took his general argument as personal advice, and I did give up my tenure at Brown. As things turned out, the Chicago debate over my tenure promotion in 1975 was sufficiently political and acrimonious (albeit eventually favorable) that I ended up leaving for the University of Rochester. Although I tried again unsuccessfully at Chicago in 1982–1984 (in a tenured position!), I think that—had I refused their inferior offer in 1973—I would probably be at Chicago today. (Whether this placement would be good for me or the profession I leave for others to decide.)

One of the best things about the University of Chicago environment is the workshop system; Milton was still running the famous Money and Banking Workshop in 1972–1975. He conducted the workshop in a "page-one/page-two" format. Instead of allowing the speaker to present the paper, Milton began by asking "Does anyone have comments on page 1?" The speaker was then allowed to respond to the comments on page 1, and so on for subsequent pages.

In a 1973 workshop, I presented my paper, published in the 1974 *Journal of Political Economy*,[12] about Ricardian equivalence for budget deficits. (In the model, taxes and budget deficits had equivalent economic effects, along the lines expressed by the classical British economist David Ricardo. However, I should mention that no one in the 1973 workshop noted the connection between my paper and Ricardo's.) This was the only time I witnessed a seminar attended simultaneously by the three great pillars of the Chicago School—Milton, George Stigler, and Gary Becker. At one point, Gary and I got involved in a heated dispute on a technical point in the paper. I recall Milton putting his head down, deep in thought for at least a full minute, while the room was silent. Given Milton's mental quickness, this prolonged deliberation was quite unusual, and there was an atmosphere of thick tension in the room. Finally, Milton lifted his head and declared, in an incredulous way, that Gary was wrong (a nearly unprecedented event) and that I was therefore right. For some reason, Gary lacks any recollection of this event.

Milton moved to San Francisco and joined Stanford University's Hoover Institution in 1977. He wrote *Memoirs* with Rose while at Hoover, and his mind remained remarkably nimble even into his nineties. On one occasion, Milton remarked how surprised he was still to be alive at such an advanced age, that somehow it was a contingency for which he had not planned. Nevertheless, we can only be grateful for this outcome.

More generally, we are fortunate that Milton had the good humor and self-confidence to persevere in the face of many years of scorn by left-wing economists and journalists. The tables were turned on his detractors many years ago, and—to paraphrase his misused quote about Keynes—we are all Friedmanians now.

Notes

[1] George Stigler, *Memoirs of an Unregulated Economist* (New York: Basic Books, 1988), p. 40.

[2] This quote is from Friedman's 1968 essay "Inflation: Causes and Consequences," *Dollars and Deficits* (Englewood Cliffs, NJ: Prentice-Hall, 1968), p. 29.

[3] Milton Friedman, "The Quantity of Money—A Restatement" in *Studies in the Quantity Theory of Money* (Chicago: University of Chicago Press, 1956); and, with Anna Jacobson Schwartz *A Monetary History of the United States* (Princeton, NJ: Princeton University Press [for the National Bureau of Economic Research], 1963).

[4] Milton Friedman, *A Theory of the Consumption Function* (Princeton, NJ: Princeton University Press, 1957).

[5] Milton Friedman, *A Program for Monetary Stability* (New York: Fordham University Press, 1960).

[6] Milton Friedman, *Essays in Positive Economics* (Chicago: University of Chicago Press, 1953).

[7] Milton Friedman, *Capitalism and Freedom* (Chicago: University of Chicago Press, 1962), pp. 1–2.

[8] Milton Friedman, with Rose Friedman, *Free to Choose* (New York: Harcourt Brace Jovanovich, 1980); and, with Rose Friedman, *Two Lucky People: Memoirs* (Chicago: University of Chicago Press, 1998), p. 501.

[9] Ibid., p. 110.

[10] Ibid., p. 363.

[11] Ibid., p. 231.

[12] Robert J. Barro, "Are Government Bonds Net Wealth?" *Journal of Political Economy* 82 (November/December, 1974): 1095–117.

DONALD J. DEVINE

Politics Trumps Economics

After Steve Forbe's brilliant defense of economic freedom that begins this volume, one might ask (in great frustration): "Since free market economists had so clearly won this 'great economic debate,' why does Washington not know it?"

I had wondered why a political scientist was being included in this volume, and now I understand only too well. Experts on economists Friedrich Hayek, Ludwig von Mises, John Maynard Keynes, Frank Knight, James Buchanan, and Milton Friedman were invited to present the good news that limited government and free market ideas were superior to their socialist alternatives and had won the day intellectually worldwide. As a political scientist, I was invited to tell the sad truth that this does not make any difference to politicians.

In the wake of the fall of communism and the worldwide movement toward markets, and led by a Republican president, Senate, and House of Representatives, nondefense, nonsecurity spending in the U.S. has increased proportionately more under George W. Bush than it had under any president since Franklin D. Roosevelt. Indeed, the current administration and Congress added the first new large entitlement since Lyndon Johnson's Great Society, the Medicare prescription drug act. As the existing entitlements are already nearing fiscal imbalance, this single act adds a liability of 150 percent to that of all of Social Security's, bringing the total unfunded liability to $50 trillion. And this was done without even a remote idea of how to pay for it. At the same time, government planning soared, as measured by the Competitive Enterprise Institute's count of regulatory additions to the *Federal Register*. Pork-generating earmarks increased from 150 in 1987—when they drew a veto from Ronald Reagan for being excessive—to 1,400 in 1998 and to 6,371 in 2005.

The sad fact of political science is that politics trumps economics—and, unfortunately, always will. Unless one adopts pure anarchism—and even Mises accepted a central role for government in regulating the police power—government rules will structure how economic affairs will operate. They might negatively affect economic activity, and economists demonstrate they often do, but Hayek was unambiguous in insisting that pure laissez-faire never was and never can be. For one thing, markets require private property and property requires legal rules under which to operate. Hayek, following John Locke, required that the rules be "promulgated, established laws, not to be varied in particular cases, but to have one rule for rich and poor" adopted by popular consent, "by themselves or their deputies," with the aim of preserving property, security, and liberty.

Once government is granted the powers to regulate policing of coercion domestically and internationally and to set the rules for property ownership, it is difficult to limit its powers to only those necessary functions. That was a major concern for the economists we have discussed, all of whom in varying degrees went beyond simple economics to matters of law and political science. Indeed, it can truly be argued that Hayek's and Buchanan's major contributions were in politics, even though they won their Nobels in the gloomy science. All of these men had wonderful ideas to limit central power but, as even the U.S. record demonstrates, they have not been embraced in the real world as have their more strictly economic insights, which have often been overridden by political considerations.

Columnist Thomas Friedman has nicely captured the difference between the two different realms with his symbols of "The Lexus and the Olive Tree." The Lexus is in the marketplace and is the domain of economics. The olive tree is a symbol of the family domicile, carefully tended and protectively surrounding loved ones, where all are safe and sound as long as the outside is kept out. But trade introduces the Lexus within the range of the garden and with it comes foreign ideas and images that threaten family and community. In response, clan or tribe or government attempt to block the intruders, who often fight back with their own governmental powers. In such an environment, few are willing to die for their Lexus, but many will die for their family and friends and olive trees, the domain of politics.

Politics trumps economics because the olive tree trumps the Lexus. I like my Lexus, but I love my family and friends. Through Machiavelli, politicians have learned to manipulate such symbols so that they can control economies and their resulting wealth, although the wise prince was warned to respect property because people will fight for their olive trees. Lobbying by businessmen will often win advantage for some market participants, and a political scientist must know this has only marginal effect. But it was not until I became personally and professionally close to a top legislative leader did I learn that, in fact, the influence is the other way around. The legislator manipulates the economic interests to support him rather than being influenced by them—at least most of the time. The politician has his ear closer to the olive tree interests, and those who will actually fight for their rights, than he does to the businessmen who, as Joseph Schumpeter noted, do not have the courage to say "boo to a goose," especially clever and powerful political ones.

A political scientist must predict that with all our greater knowledge of and respect for the market, the economy will get worse because of politics, but especially because of today's realities. The bills for years of political irresponsibility on entitlements will become due as early as 2016, and tax rates will have to increase greatly to pay them. By 2030, Medicare and Social Security will absorb 14 percent of GDP, almost half of it unfunded, requiring a 91 percent increase in the payroll tax, or an 81 percent increase in income taxes, or a 36 percent increase in total federal taxes. This will drastically slow growth, if it does not lead to hyperinflation or depression. As these obligations come due, fewer workers will be available to pay them. There are fewer younger workers available to take the place of the now less productive elderly; and the younger works are having fewer children to eventually support their own retirement.

It takes 2.1 children per childbearing-aged woman to keep the population steady. Europe is already finished. The birth rate is down to 1.4 percent there and heading lower, which soon will lead to depopulation or mass immigration. The U.S. is doing better at 2.0 children per childbearing-aged woman, but only 1.8 for the segment of the population that is of European descent. The immigration that is mitigating the decline in U.S. population to some extent, however, already has created a backlash that might make the demographic problem worse. The geopolitical aspects of the shift might even be greater. Of the 43 countries that will be dealing with declining populations in the next 50 years, 80 percent are European and none are Muslim. Of the ten countries with the world's largest populations today, none are Islamic; but by 2030, half will be. The United States will decrease from 6.3 percent of the world population today to 4.6 percent in 2050, while the world's Muslim population will increase by 100 percent.

No politician is allowed to discuss the coming entitlements-based crisis even though it will begin in less than a decade. Although President Bush raised the idea of Social Security reform, he was stopped cold last year, in fact he was jeered when he mentioned it in his 2006 State of the Union address. The Medicare problems, which are much larger problems, can be discussed by no one. In fact, politicians mostly call for increased taxes, less free trade, more regulation, and additional spending—including President Bush's own incredibly expensive new prescription drug entitlement. At a press conference just before the State of the Union, President Bush declared himself satisfied with the rate of spending under the current Congress, saying it had met his targets (if not his budgets) and that he did not foresee any future vetoes.

Can the coming entitlement crash be avoided if it cannot be discussed? What about birth replacement rates? Try telling American young men and women they must have 2.1 children per family: This would mean three children for most young families—and four or more children in many others to make up for those who do not marry or who prefer the same sex. Medicare reform would seem an easy sell by comparison. If the population were convinced of the need to become more traditionally religious that might help since, as even nonbeliever Hayek said, paradoxically, freedom and markets require a traditional society with traditional moral values developed in sound families and vibrant local communities. Good luck selling that to the Paris Hilton generation.

The specter of politics-future trumps the economic good news that the market has won intellectually. It would take a moral transformation of gargantuan proportions to change these social dynamics. One should urge the new generation to find a way anyway—and the eternal optimist Ronald Reagan would be the soundest guide. But preaching a politics of restraint is not as easy as teaching economics with a Lexus as the prize.

LUDWIG VON MISES

LORD KEYNES AND SAY'S LAW

I

Lord Keynes's main contribution did not lie in the development of new ideas but "in escaping from the old ones," as he himself declared at the end of the Preface to his "General Theory." The Keynesians tell us that his immortal achievement consists in the entire refutation of what has come to be known as Say's Law of Markets. The rejection of this law, they declare, is the gist of all Keynes's teachings; all other propositions of his doctrine follow with logical necessity from this fundamental insight and must collapse if the futility of his attack on Say's Law can be demonstrated.[1]

Now it is important to realize that what is called Say's Law was in the first instance designed as a refutation of doctrines popularly held in the ages preceding the development of economics as a branch of human knowledge. It was not an integral part of the new science of economics as taught by the Classical economists. It was rather a preliminary—the exposure and removal of garbled and untenable ideas which dimmed people's minds and were a serious obstacle to a reasonable analysis of conditions.

Whenever business turned bad, the average merchant had two explanations at hand: the evil was caused by a scarcity of money and

---

Reprinted courtesy of the Ludwig von Mises Institute (www.mises.org). Originally published in *The Freeman*, October 30, 1950, and reprinted in *Planning for Freedom*.

by general overproduction. Adam Smith, in a famous passage in *The Wealth of Nations*, exploded the first of these myths. Say devoted himself predominantly to a thorough refutation of the second.

As long as a definite thing is still an economic good and not a "free good," its supply is not, of course, *absolutely* abundant. There are still unsatisfied needs which a larger supply of the good concerned could satisfy. There are still people who would be glad to get more of this good than they are really getting. With regard to economic goods there can never be *absolute* overproduction. (And economics deals only with economic goods, not with free goods such as air which are no object of purposive human action, are therefore not produced, and with regard to which the employment of terms like underproduction and overproduction is simply nonsensical.)

With regard to economic goods there can be only *relative* overproduction. While the consumers are asking for definite quantities of shirts and of shoes, business has produced, say, a larger quantity of shoes and a smaller quantity of shirts. This is not general overproduction of all commodities. To the overproduction of shoes corresponds an underproduction of shirts. Consequently the result cannot be a general depression of all branches of business. The outcome is a change in the exchange ratio between shoes and shirts. If, for instance, previously one pair of shoes could buy four shirts, it now buys only three shirts. While business is bad for the shoemakers, it is good for the shirtmakers. The attempts to explain the general depression of trade by referring to an allegedly general overproduction are therefore fallacious.

Commodities, says Say, are ultimately paid for not by money, but by other commodities. Money is merely the commonly used medium of exchange; it plays only an intermediary role. What the seller wants ultimately to receive in exchange for the commodities sold is other commodities.

Every commodity produced is therefore a price, as it were, for other commodities produced. The situation of the producer of any commodity is improved by any increase in the production of other commodities. What may hurt the interests of the producer of a definite commodity is his failure to anticipate correctly the state of the market. He has overrated the public's demand for his commodity and underrated its demand for other commodities. Consumers have no use for such a bungling entrepreneur; they buy his products only at prices which make him incur losses, and they force him, if he does not in time correct his mistakes, to go out of business. On the other hand, those entrepreneurs who have better succeeded in anticipating the public demand earn profits and are in a position to expand their business activities. This, says Say, is the truth behind the confused assertions of businessmen that the main difficulty is not in producing but in selling. It would be more appropriate to declare that the first and main problem of business is to produce in the best and cheapest way those commodities which will satisfy the most urgent of the not yet satisfied needs of the public.

Thus Smith and Say demolished the oldest and most naive explanation of the trade cycle as provided by the popular effusions of inefficient traders. True, their achievement was merely negative. They exploded the belief that the recurrence of periods of bad business was caused by a scarcity of money and by a general overproduction. But they did not give us an elaborated theory of the trade cycle. The first explanation of this phenomenon was provided much later by the British Currency School.

The important contributions of Smith and Say were not entirely new and original. The history of economic thought can trace back some essential points of their reasoning to older authors. This in no way detracts from the merits of Smith and Say. They were the first to deal with the issue in a systematic way and to apply their conclusions to the problem of economic depressions. They were therefore also the first against whom the supporters of the spurious popular doctrine directed their violent attacks. Sismondi and Malthus chose Say as the target of passionate volleys when they tried—in vain—to salvage the discredited popular prejudices.

II

Say emerged victoriously from his polemics with Malthus and Sismondi. He proved his case, while his adversaries could not prove theirs. Henceforth, during the whole rest of the nineteenth century, the acknowledgment of the truth contained in Say's Law was the distinctive mark of an economist. Those authors and politicians who made the alleged scarcity of money responsible for all ills and advocated inflation as the panacea were no longer considered economists but "monetary cranks."

The struggle between the champions of sound money and the inflationists went on for many decades. But it was no longer considered a controversy between various schools of economists. It was viewed as a conflict between economists and anti-economists, between reasonable men and ignorant zealots. When all civilized countries had adopted the gold standard or the gold-exchange standard, the cause of inflation seemed to be lost forever.

Economics did not content itself with what Smith and Say had taught about the problems involved. It developed an integrated system of theorems which cogently demonstrated the absurdity of the inflationist sophisms. It depicted in detail the inevitable consequences of an increase in the quantity of money in circulation and of credit expansion. It elaborated the monetary or circulation credit theory of the business cycle which clearly showed how the recurrence of depressions of trade is caused by the repeated attempts to "stimulate" business through credit expansion. Thus it conclusively proved that the slump, whose appearance the inflationists attributed to an insufficiency of the supply of money, is on the contrary the necessary outcome of attempts to remove such an alleged scarcity of money through credit expansion.

The economists did not contest the fact that a credit expansion in its initial stage makes business boom. But they pointed out how such a contrived boom must inevitably collapse after a while and produce a general depression. This demonstration could appeal to statesmen intent on promoting the enduring well-being of their nation. It could not influence demagogues who care for nothing but success in the impending election campaign and are not in the least troubled about what will happen the day after tomorrow. But it is precisely such people who have become supreme in the political life of this age of wars and revolutions. In defiance of all the teachings of the economists, inflation and credit expansion have been elevated to the dignity of the first principle of economic policy. Nearly all governments are now committed to reckless spending, and finance their deficits by issuing additional quantities of unredeemable paper money and by boundless credit expansion.

The great economists were harbingers of new ideas. The economic policies they recommended were at variance with the policies practiced by contemporary governments and political parties. As a rule many years, even decades, passed before public opinion accepted the new ideas as propagated by the economists, and before the required corresponding changes in policies were effected.

It was different with the "new economics" of Lord Keynes. The policies he advocated were precisely those which almost all governments, including the British, had already adopted many years before his "General Theory" was published. Keynes was not an innovator and champion of new methods of managing economic affairs. His contribution consisted rather in providing an apparent justification for the policies which were popular with those in power in spite of the fact that all economists viewed them as disastrous. His achievement was a rationalization of the policies already practiced. He was not a "revolutionary," as some of his adepts called him. The "Keynesian revolution" took place long before Keynes approved of it and fabricated a pseudo-scientific justification for it. What he really did was to write an apology for the prevailing policies of governments.

This explains the quick success of his book. It was greeted enthusiastically by the governments and the ruling political parties. Especially enraptured were a new type of intellectual, the "government economists." They had had a bad conscience. They were aware of the fact that they were carrying out policies which all economists condemned as contrary to purpose and disastrous. Now they felt relieved. The "new economics" reestablished their moral equilibrium. Today they are no longer ashamed of being the handymen of bad policies. They glorify themselves. They are the prophets of the new creed.

III

The exuberant epithets which these admirers have bestowed upon his work cannot obscure the fact that Keynes did not refute Say's Law. He rejected it emotionally, but he did not advance a single tenable argument to invalidate its rationale.

Neither did Keynes try to refute by discursive reasoning the teachings of modern economics. He chose to ignore them, that was all. He never found any word of serious criticism against the theorem that increasing the quantity of money cannot effect anything else than, on the one hand, to favor some groups at the expense of other groups, and, on the other hand, to foster capital malinvestment and capital decumulation. He was at a complete loss when it came to advancing any sound argument to demolish the monetary theory of the trade cycle. All he did was to revive the self-contradictory dogmas of the various sects of inflationism. He did not add anything to the empty presumptions of his predecessors, from the old Birmingham School of Little Shilling Men down to Silvio Gesell. He merely translated their sophisms—a hundred times refuted—into the questionable language of mathematical economics. He passed over in silence all the objections which such men as Jevons, Walras, and Wicksell— to name only a few—opposed to the effusions of the inflationists.

It is the same with his disciples. They think that calling "those who fail to be moved to admiration of Keynes's genius" such names as "dullard" or "narrow-minded fanatic"[2] is a substitute for sound economic reasoning. They believe that they have proved their case by dismissing their adversaries as "orthodox" or "neo-classical." They reveal the utmost ignorance in thinking that their doctrine is correct because it is new.

In fact, inflationism is the oldest of all fallacies. It was very popular long before the days of Smith, Say, and Ricardo, against whose teachings the Keynesians cannot advance any other objection than that they are old.

IV

The unprecedented success of Keynesianism is due to the fact that it provides an apparent justification for the "deficit spending" policies of contemporary governments. It is the pseudo-philosophy of those who can think of nothing else than to dissipate the capital accumulated by previous generations.

Yet no effusions of authors however brilliant and sophisticated can alter the perennial economic laws. They are and work and take care of themselves. Notwithstanding all the passionate fulminations of the spokesmen of governments, the inevitable consequences of inflationism and expansionism as depicted by the "orthodox" economists are coming to pass. And then, very late indeed, even simple people will discover that Keynes did not teach us how to perform the "miracle ... of turning a stone into bread,"[3] but the not at all miraculous procedure of eating the seed corn.

Notes

[1] P. M. Sweezy in *The New Economics*, ed. by S. E. Harris, New York, 1947, p. 105.
[2] Professor G. Haberler in ibid., p. 161
[3] John Maynard Keynes in ibid., p. 332.

LUDWIG VON MISES

ECONOMIC ASPECTS OF THE PENSION PROBLEM

On Whom Does the Incidence Fall?

Whenever a law or labor union pressure burdens the employers with an additional expenditure for the benefit of the employees, people talk of "social gains." The idea implied is that such benefits confer on the employees a boon beyond the salaries or wages paid to them and that they are receiving a grant which they would have missed in the absence of such a law or such a clause in the contract. It is assumed that the workers are getting something for nothing.

This view is entirely fallacious. What the employer takes into account in considering the employment of additional hands or in discharging a number of those already in his service, is always the value of the services rendered or to be rendered by them. He asks himself: How much does the employment of the man concerned add to the output? Is it reasonable to expect that the expenditure caused by his employment will at least be recovered by the sale of the additional product produced by his employment? If the answer to the second question is in the negative, the employment of the man will cause a loss. As no enterprise can in the long run operate on a loss basis, the man concerned will be discharged or, respectively, will not be hired.

Reprinted courtesy of the Ludwig von Mises Institute (www.mises.org). From the *The Commercial and Financial Chronicle*, February 23, 1950.

In resorting to this calculation, the employer takes into account not only the individual's take-home wages, but all the costs of employing him. If, for example, the government—as is the case in some European countries—collects a percentage of each firm's total payroll as a tax which the firm is strictly forbidden to deduct from wages paid to the workers, the amount that enters into the calculation is: wages paid out to the worker plus the quota of the tax. If the employer is bound to provide for pensions, the sum entered into the calculation is: wages paid out plus an allowance for the pension, computed according to actuarial methods.

The consequence of this state of affairs is that the incidence of all alleged "social gains" falls upon the wage-earner. Their effect does not differ from the effect of any kind of raise in wage rates.

In a free labor market, wage rates tend toward a height at which all employers ready to pay these rates can find all the men they need and all the workers ready to work for this rate can find jobs. There prevails a tendency toward full employment. But as soon as the laws or the labor unions fix rates at a higher level, this tendency disappears. Then workers are discharged and there are job-seekers who cannot find employment. The reason is that at the artificially raised wage rates only the employment of a smaller number of hands pays. While in an unhampered labor market unemployment is only transitory, it becomes a permanent phenomenon when the governments or the unions succeed in raising wage rates above the potential market level. Even Lord Beveridge, about twenty years ago, admitted that the continuance of a substantial volume of unemployment is in itself the proof that the price asked for labor as wages is too high for the conditions of the market. And Lord Keynes, the inaugurator of the so-called "full employment policy," implicitly acknowledged the correctness of this thesis. His main reason for advocating inflation as a means to do away with unemployment was that he believed that gradual and automatic lowering of real wages as a result of rising prices would not be so strongly resisted by labor as any attempt to lower money wage rates.

What prevents the government and the unions from raising wage rates to a steeper height than they actually do is their reluctance to price out of the labor market too great a number of people. What the workers are getting in the shape of pensions payable by the employing corporation reduces the amount of wages that the unions can ask for without increasing unemployment. The unions in asking pensions for which the company has to pay without any contribution on the part of the beneficiaries has made a choice. It has preferred pensions to an increase in take-home wages. Economically it does not make any difference whether the workers do contribute or do not to the fund out of which the pensions will be paid. It is immaterial for the employer whether the cost of employing workers is raised by an increase in take-home wages or by the obligation to provide for pensions. For the worker, on the other hand, the pensions are not a free gift on the part of the employer. The pension claims they acquire restrict the amount of wages they could get without calling up the spectre of unemployment.

Correctly computed, the income of a wage earner entitled to a pension consists of his wages plus the amount of the premium he would have to pay to an insurance company for the acquisition of an equivalent claim. Ultimately the granting of pensions amounts to a restriction of the wage earner's freedom to use his total income according to his own designs. He is forced to cut down his current consumption in order to provide for his old age. We may neglect dealing with the question whether such a restriction of the individual worker's freedom is expedient or not. What is important to emphasize is merely that the pensions are not a gift on the part of the employer. They are a disguised wage raise of a peculiar character. The employee is forced to use the increment for acquiring a pension.

Pensions and the Purchasing Power of the Dollar

It is obvious that the amount of the pension each man will be entitled to claim one day can only be fixed in terms of money. Hence the value of these claims is inextricably linked with the vicissitudes of the American monetary unit, the dollar.

The present Administration is eager to devise various schemes for old-age and disability pensions. It is intent upon extending the number of people included in the government's social security system and to increase the benefits under this system. It openly supports the demands of the unions for pensions to be granted by the companies without contribution on the part of the beneficiaries. But at the same time the same administration is firmly committed to a policy which is bound to lower more and more the purchasing power of the dollar. It has proclaimed unbalanced budgets and deficit spending as the first principle of public finance, as a new way of life. While hypocritically pretending to fight inflation, it has elevated boundless credit expansion and recklessly increasing the amount of money in circulation to the dignity of an essential postulate of popular government and economic democracy.

Let nobody be fooled by the lame excuse that what is intended is not permanent deficits, but only the substitution of balancing the budget over a period of several years for balancing it every year. According to this doctrine, in years of prosperity budgetary surpluses are to be accumulated which have to be balanced against the deficits incurred in years of depression. But what is to be considered as good business and what as bad business is left to the decision of the party in power. The Administration itself declared that the fiscal year 1949 was, in spite of a moderate recession near its end, a year of prosperity. But it did not accumulate a surplus in this year of prosperity; it produced a considerable deficit. Remember how the Democrats in the 1932 electoral campaign criticized the Hoover Administration for its financial shortcomings. But as soon as they came into office, they inaugurated their notorious schemes of pump-priming, deficit spending, and so on.

What the doctrine of balancing budgets over a period of many years really means is this: as long as our own party is in office, we will enhance our popularity through reckless spending. We do not want to annoy our friends by cutting down expenditure. We want the voters to feel happy under the artificial short-lived prosperity which the easy money policy and a rich supply of additional money generate. Later, when our adversaries will be in office, the inevitable consequence of our expansionist policy, viz., depression, will appear. Then we shall blame them for the disaster and assail them for their failure to balance the budget properly.

It is very unlikely that the practice of deficit spending will be abandoned in the not too distant future. As a fiscal policy it is very convenient to inept governments. It is passionately advocated by hosts of pseudo-economists. It is praised at the universities as the most beneficial expedient of "unorthodox," really "progressive" and "anti-fascist" methods of public finance. A radical change of ideologies would be required to restore the prestige of sound fiscal procedures, today decried as "orthodox" and "reactionary."

Such an overthrow of an almost universally accepted doctrine is unlikely to occur as long as the living generation of professors and politicians has not passed away. The present writer, having for more than forty years uncompromisingly fought against all varieties of credit expansion and inflation, is forced sadly to admit that the prospects for a speedy return to sound management of monetary affairs are rather thin. A realistic evaluation of the state of public opinion, the doctrines taught at the universities and the mentality of politicians and pressure groups must show us that the inflationist tendencies will prevail for many years.

The inevitable result of inflationary policies is a drop in the monetary unit's purchasing power. Compare the dollar of 1950 with the dollar of 1940! Compare the money of any European or American country with its nominal equivalent a dozen or two dozen years ago! As an inflationary policy works only as long as the yearly increments in the amount of money in circulation are increased more and more, the rise in prices and wages and the corresponding drop in purchasing power will go on at an accelerated pace. The experience of the French franc may give us a rough image of the dollar thirty or forty years from today.

Now it is such periods of time that count for pension plans. The present workers of the United States Steel Corporation will receive their pensions in twenty, thirty, or forty years. Today a pension of one hundred dollars a month means a rather substantial allowance. What will it mean in 1980 or 1990? Today, as the Welfare Commissioner of the City of New York has shown, 52 cents can buy all the food a person needs to meet the daily caloric and protein requirements. How much will 52 cents buy in 1980? [Editor: 0.17 cent.]

Such is the issue. What the workers are aiming at in striving after social security and pensions is, of course, security. But their "social gain" withers away with the drop in the dollar's purchasing power. In enthusiastically supporting the Fair Deal's fiscal policy, the union members are themselves frustrating all their social security and pension schemes. The pensions they will be entitled one day to claim will be a mere sham.

No solution can be found for this dilemma. In an industrial society all deferred payments must be stipulated in terms of money. They shrink with the shrinking of the money's purchasing power. A policy of deficit spending saps the very foundation of all interpersonal relations and contracts. It frustrates all kinds of savings, social security benefits, and pensions.

Pensions and the "New Economics"

How can it happen that the American workers fail to see that their policies are at cross purposes?

The answer is: they are deluded by the fallacies of what is called "new economics." This allegedly new philosophy ignores the role of capital accumulation. It does not realize that there is but one means to increase wage rates for all those eager to get jobs and thereby to improve the standard of living, namely to accelerate the increase of capital as compared with population. It talks about technological progress and productivity without being aware that no technological improvement can be achieved if the capital required is lacking. Just at the instant in which it became obvious that the most serious obstacle to any further economic betterment is not only in the backward countries but also in England, the shortage of capital.

Lord Keynes, enthusiastically supported by many American authors, advanced his doctrine of the evils of saving and capital accumulation. As these men see it, all that is unsatisfactory is caused by the inability of private enterprise to cope with the conditions of the "mature" economy. The remedy they recommend is simple indeed. The state should fill the gap. They blithely assume that the state has unlimited means at its disposal. The state can undertake all projects which are too big for private capital. There is simply nothing that would surpass the financial power of the government of the United States. The Tennessee Valley project and the Marshall plan were just modest beginnings. There are still many valleys in America left for further action. And then there are many rivers in other parts of the globe. Only a short time ago Senator McMahon outlined a gigantic project that dwarfs the Marshall plan. Why not? If it is unnecessary to adjust the amount of expenditure to the means available, there is no limit to the spending of the great god State.

It is no wonder that the common man falls prey to the illusions which dim the vision of dignified statesmen and learned professors. Like the expert advisers of the President, he entirely neglects to recognize the main problem of American business, viz., the insufficiency of the accumulation of new capital. He dreams of abundance while a shortage is threatening. He misinterprets the high profits which the companies report. He does not perceive that a considerable part of these profits are illusory, a mere arithmetical consequence of the fact that the sums laid aside as depreciation quotas are insufficient. These illusory profits, a phony result of the drop in the dollar's purchasing power, will be absorbed by the already risen costs of replacing the factories' worn-out equipment. Their ploughing back is not additional investment, it is merely capital maintenance. There is much less available for a substantial expansion of investment and for the improvement of technological methods than the misinformed public thinks.

Looking backward fifty or a hundred years we observe a steady progress of America's ability to produce and thereby to consume. But it is a serious blunder to assume that this trend is bound to continue. This past progress has been effected by a speedy increase of capital accumulation. If the accumulation of new capital is slowed down or entirely ceases, there cannot be any question of further improvements.

Such is the real problem American labor has to face today. The problems of capital maintenance and the accumulation of new capital do not concern merely "management." They are vital for the wage earner. Exclusively preoccupied with wage rates and pensions, the unions boast of their Pyrrhic victories. The union members are not conscious of the fact that their fate is tied up with the flowering of their employers' enterprises. As voters they approve of a taxation system which taxes away and dissipates for current expenditure those funds which would have been saved and invested as new capital.

What the workers must learn is that the only reason why wage rates are higher in the United States than in other countries is that the per head quota of capital invested is higher. The psychological danger of all kinds of pension plans is to be seen in the fact that they obscure this point. They give to the workers an unfounded feeling of security. Now, they think, our future is safe. No need to worry any longer. The unions will win for us more and more social gains. An age of plenty is in sight.

Yet, the workers should be worried about the state of the supply of capital. They should be worried because the preservation and the further improvement of what is called "the American way of life" and "an American standard of living" depends on the maintenance and the further increase of the capital invested in American business.

A man who is forced to provide of his own account for his old age must save a part of his income or take out an insurance policy. This leads him to examine the financial status of the savings bank or the insurance company or the soundness of the bonds he buys. Such a man is more likely to get an idea of the economic problems of his country than a man whom a pension scheme seemingly relieves of all worries. He will get the incentive to read the financial page of his newspaper and will become interested in articles which thoughtless people skip. If he is keen enough he will discover the flaw in the teachings of the "new economics."

But the man who confides in the pension stipulated believes that all such issues are "mere theory" and do not affect him. He does not bother about those things on which his well-being depends because he ignores this dependence. As citizens such people are a liability. A nation cannot prosper if its members are not fully aware of the fact that what alone can improve their conditions is more and better production. And this can only be brought about by increased saving and capital accumulation.

LUDWIG VON MISES

LAISSEZ FAIRE OR DICTATORSHIP

1. What the Encyclopaedia of the Social Sciences says about Laissez Faire

For more than a hundred years the maxim *laissez faire, laissez passer* has been a red rag to harbingers of totalitarian despotism. As these zealots see it, this maxim condenses all the shameful principles of capitalism. To unmask its fallacies is therefore tantamount to exploding the ideological foundations of the system of private ownership of the means of production, and implicitly demonstrating the excellence of its antithesis, viz., communism and socialism.

The *Encyclopaedia of the Social Sciences* may fairly be considered as representative of the doctrines taught at American and British universities and colleges. Its ninth volume contains an article, "Laissez Faire," from the pen of the Oxford professor and author of detective stories, G. D. H. Cole. In the five and a quarter pages of his contribution Professor Cole freely indulges in the use of deprecatory epithets. The maxim "cannot stand examination," it is only prevalent in "popular economics," it is "theoretically bankrupt," an "anachronism," it survives only as a "prejudice," but "as a doctrine deserving of theoretical respect it is dead." Resort to these and many other similar opprobrious appellations fails to disguise the fact that Professor Cole's arguments entirely miss the point. Professor Cole is

Reprinted courtesy of the Ludwig von Mises Institute (www.mises.org). The following essay originally appeared in *Plain Talk* 3(4; January 1949): 57–64.

not qualified to deal with the problems involved because he simply does not know what the market economy is and how it works. The only correct affirmation of his article is the truism that those rejecting laissez faire are Socialists. He is also right in declaring that the refutation of laissez faire is "as prominent in the national idea of Fascism in Italy as in Russian Communism."

The volume which contains Mr. Cole's article was published in January 1933. This explains why he did not include Nazi Germany in the ranks of those nations which have freed themselves from the spell of the sinister maxim. He merely registers with satisfaction that the conception rejecting laissez faire is "at the back of many projects of national planning which, largely under Russian influence, is now being put forward all over the world."

2. Laissez Faire Means Free Market Economy

Learned historians have bestowed much pains upon the question to whom the origin of the maxim *laissez faire, laissez passer* is to be attributed.[1] At any rate it is certain that in the second part of the eighteenth century the outstanding French champions of economic freedom—foremost among them Gournay, Quesnay, Turgot, and Mirabeau—compressed their program for popular use into this sentence. Their aim was the establishment of the unhampered market economy. In order to attain this end they advocated the abolition of all statutes preventing the more industrious and more efficient people from outdoing the less industrious and less efficient competitors and restricting the mobility of commodities and of men. It was this that the famous maxim was designed to express.

In occasionally using the words *laissez faire, laissez passer,* the eighteenth-century economists did not intend to baptize their social philosophy the laissez faire doctrine. They concentrated their efforts upon the elaboration of a new system of social and political ideas which would benefit mankind. They were not eager to organize a faction or party and to find a name for it. It was only later, in the second decade of the nineteenth century, that a term came to signify the total complex of the political philosophy of freedom, viz., liberalism. The new word was borrowed from Spain where it designated the friends of constitutional government and religious freedom. Very soon it was used all over Europe as a label for the endeavors of those who stood for representative government; freedom of thought, of speech and of the press; private ownership of the means of production; and free trade.

The liberal program is an indivisible and indissoluble whole, not an arbitrarily assembled patchwork of diverse components. Its various parts condition one another. The idea that political freedom can be preserved in the absence of economic freedom, and vice versa, is an illusion. Political freedom is the corollary of economic freedom. It is no accident that the age of capitalism became also the age of government by the people. If individuals are not free to buy and to sell on the market, they turn into virtual slaves dependent on the good graces of the omnipotent government, whatever the wording of the constitution may be.

The fathers of socialism and modern interventionism were fully aware that their own programs were incompatible with the political postulates of liberalism. The main target of their passionate attacks was liberalism as a whole. They did not make a distinction between the political and the economic aspects of liberalism.

But as the years went on, the Socialists and interventionists of the Anglo-Saxon countries discovered that it was a hopeless venture to attack liberalism and the idea of liberty openly. The prestige of liberal institutions was so overwhelming in the English-speaking world, that no party could risk defying them directly. Anti-liberalism's only chance was to camouflage itself as true and genuine liberalism and to denounce the attitudes of all other parties as a mere counterfeit liberalism.

The continental Socialists had fanatically smeared and disparaged liberalism and progressivism, and contemptuously derogated democracy as "pluto-democracy." Their Anglo-Saxon imitators, who at first had adopted the same procedure, after a while reversed their semantics and arrogated to themselves the appellations liberal, progressive, and democratic. They began flatly to deny that political freedom is the corollary of economic freedom. They boldly asserted that democratic institutions can work satisfactorily only where the government has full control of all production activities and the individual citizen is bound to obey unconditionally all orders issued by the central planning board. In their eyes all-round regimentation is the only means to make people free, and freedom of the press is best guaranteed by a government monopoly of printing and publishing. They were not plagued by any scruples when they stole the good old name of liberalism and began to call their own tenets and policies liberal. In this country the term "liberalism" is nowadays more often than not used as a synonym for communism.

The semantic innovation which the Socialists and interventionists thus inaugurated left the advocates of freedom without any name. There was no term available to call those who believe that private ownership of the material factors of production is the best, in fact, the only means to make the nation and all its individual citizens as prosperous as possible and to make representative government work. The Socialists and interventionists believe that such people do not deserve any name, but are to be referred to only by such insulting epithets as "economic royalists," "Wall Street sycophants," "reactionaries," and so on.

This state of affairs explains why the phrase laissez faire was more and more used to signify the ideas of those who advocate the free market economy as against government planning and regimentation.

3. The Cairnes Argument against Laissez Faire

Today it is no longer difficult for intelligent men to realize that the alternative is market economy or communism. Production can either be directed by buying and abstention from buying on the part of all people, or it can be directed by the orders of the supreme chief of state. Men must choose between these two systems of society's economic organization. There is no third solution, no middle way.

It is a sad fact that not only politicians and demagogues have failed to see this essential truth, but that even some economists have erred in dealing with the problems involved.

There is no need to dwell upon the unfortunate influence which originated from John Stuart Mill's confused treatment of government interference with business. It becomes evident from Mill's *Autobiography* that his change of mind resulting in what he calls "a greater approximation . . . to a qualified socialism"[2] was motivated by purely personal feelings and affections and not by emotionally undisturbed reasoning. It is certainly one of the tasks of economics to refute the errors which deform the disquisitions of so eminent a thinker as Mill. But it is unnecessary to argue against the prepossessions of Mr. Mill.

A few years after Mill, another outstanding economist, J. E. Cairnes, dealt with the same problem.[3] As a philosopher and essayist Mill by far supersedes Cairnes. But as an economist Cairnes was not second to Mill, and his contributions to the epistemology of the social sciences are of incomparably greater value and importance than those of Mill. Yet, Cairnes's analysis of laissez faire does not display that brilliant precision of reasoning which is the distinguishing mark of his other writings. As Cairnes sees it, the assertion implied in the doctrine of laissez faire is that "the promptings of self-interest will lead individuals, in all that range of their conduct which has to do with their material well-being, spontaneously to follow that course which is most for their own good and for the good of all." This assertion, he says, involves the two following assumptions: first, that the interests of human beings are fundamentally the same that what is most for my interest is also most for the interest of other people; and, secondly, that individuals know their interests in the sense in which they are coincident with the interests of others, and that, in the absence of coercion, they will in this sense follow them. If these two propositions be made out, the policy of laissez faire . . . follows with scientific rigour.

Cairnes is disposed to accept the first—the major—premise of the syllogism, that the interests of human beings are fundamentally the same. But he rejects the second—the minor—premise.[4] "Human beings know and follow their interests according to their lights and dispositions; but not necessarily, nor in practice always, in the sense in which the interest of the individual is coincident with that of others and of the whole."[5]

Let us for the sake of argument accept the way in which Cairnes presents the problem and in which he argues. Human beings are fallible and therefore sometimes fail to learn what their true interests would require them to do. Furthermore, there are "such things in the world as passion, prejudice, custom, *esprit de corps,* class interest, to draw people aside from the pursuit of their interests in the largest and highest sense."[6] It is very unfortunate that reality is such. But, we must ask, is there any means available to prevent mankind from being hurt by people's bad judgment and malice? Is it not a non sequitur to assume that one could avoid the disastrous consequences of these human weaknesses by substituting the government's discretion for that of the individual citizens? Are governments endowed with intellectual and moral perfection? Are the rulers not human too, not themselves subject to human frailties and deficiencies?

The theocratic doctrine is consistent in attributing to the head of the government superhuman powers. The French royalists contend that the solemn consecration at Rheims conveys to the King of France, anointed with the sacred oil which a dove from Heaven brought down for the consecration of Clovis, divine dispensation. The legitimate king cannot err and cannot do wrong, and his royal touch miraculously cures scrofula. No less consistent was the late German Professor Werner Sombart in declaring that *Führertum* is a permanent revelation and that the *Führer* gets his orders directly from God, the supreme *Führer* of the Universe.[7] Once you admit these premises, you can no longer raise any objections against planning and socialism. Why tolerate the incompetence of clumsy and ill-intentioned bunglers if you can be made happy and prosperous by the God-sent authority?

But Cairnes is not prepared to accept "the principle of State control, the doctrine of paternal government."[8] His disquisitions peter out in vague and contradictory talk that leaves the relevant question unanswered. He does not comprehend that it is indispensable to choose between the supremacy of individuals and that of the government. Some agency must determine how the factors of production should be employed and what should be produced. If it is not the consumer, by means of buying and abstention from buying on the market, it must be the government by compulsion.

If one rejects laissez faire on account of man's fallibility and moral weakness, one must for the same reasons also reject every kind of government action. Cairnes's mode of arguing, provided it is not integrated into a theocratic philosophy in the manner of the French royalists or the German Nazis, leads to complete anarchism and nihilism.

One of the distortions to which the self-styled "Progressives" resort in smearing laissez faire is the statement that consistent application of laissez faire must result in anarchy. There is no need to dwell upon this fallacy. It is more important to stress the fact that Cairnes's argument against laissez faire, when consistently carried through to its inevitable logical consequences, is essentially anarchistic.

4. "Conscious Planning" versus "Automatic Forces"

As the self-styled "Progressives" see things, the alternative is: "automatic forces" or "conscious planning."[9] It is obvious, they go on saying, that to rely upon automatic processes is sheer stupidity. No reasonable man can seriously recommend doing nothing and letting things go without any interference through purposive action. A plan, by the very fact that it is a display of conscious action, is incomparably superior to the absence of any planning. Laissez faire means: let evils last and do not try to improve the lot of mankind by reasonable action.

This is utterly fallacious and deceptive talk. The argument advanced for planning is derived entirely from an inadmissable interpretation of a metaphor. It has no foundation other than the connotations implied in the term "automatic," which is customarily applied in a metaphorical sense to describe the market process. Automatic, says the *Concise Oxford Dictionary*, means "unconscious, unintelligent, merely mechanical." Automatic, says *Webster's Collegiate Dictionary*, means "not subject to the control of the will . . . performed without active thought and without conscious intention or direction." What a triumph for the champion of planning to play this trump card!

The truth is that the choice is not between a dead mechanism and a rigid automatism on the one hand and conscious planning on the other hand. The alternative is not plan or no plan. The question is: whose planning? Should each member of society plan for himself or should the paternal government alone plan for all? The issue is not automatism *versus conscious action;* it is *spontaneous action of each individual versus the exclusive action of the* government. It is *freedom versus government omnipotence.*

Laissez faire does not mean: let soulless mechanical forces operate. It means: let individuals choose how they want to cooperate in the social division of labor and let them determine what the entrepreneurs should produce. Planning means: let the government alone choose and enforce its rulings by the apparatus of coercion and compulsion.

5. The Satisfaction of Man's "True" Needs

Under laissez faire, says the planner, the goods produced are not those which people "really" need, but those goods from the sale of which the highest returns are expected. It is the objective of planning to direct production toward the satisfaction of "true" needs. But who should decide what "true" needs are?

Thus, for instance, Professor Harold Laski, the former chairman of the British Labor Party, determined the objective of planned direction of investment as "the use of the investor's savings will be in housing rather than in cinemas."[10] It does not matter whether or not one agrees with the professor's personal view that better houses are more important than moving pictures. The fact is that consumers, by spending part of their money for admission to the movies, have made another choice. If the masses of Great Britain, the same people whose votes swept the Labor Party into power, were to stop patronizing the moving pictures and to spend more for comfortable homes and apartments, profit-seeking business would be forced to invest more in building homes and apartment houses, and less in the production of swanky pictures. What Professor Laski aimed at is to defy the wishes of the consumers and to substitute his own will for theirs. He wanted to do away with the democracy of the market and to establish the absolute rule of a production czar. He might pretend that he is right from a "higher" point of view, and that as a superman he is called upon to impose his own set of values on the masses of inferior men. But then he should have been frank enough to say so plainly.

All this passionate praise of the super-eminence of government action is merely a poor disguise for the individual interventionist's self-deification. The Great God State is great only because it is expected to do exclusively what the individual advocate of interventionism wants to be achieved. The only true plan is the one of which the individual planner fully approves. All other plans are simply counterfeit. What the author of a book on the benefits of planning has in mind is, of course, always his own plan alone. No planner was ever shrewd enough to consider the possibility that the plan which the government will put into practice could differ from his own plan.

The various planners agree only with regard to their rejection of laissez faire, i.e., the individual's discretion to choose and to act. They disagree entirely on the choice of the unique plan to be adopted. To every exposure of the manifest and incontestable defects of interventionist policies the champions of interventionism always react in the same way. These faults, they say, were the sins of spurious interventionism; what we are advocating is good interventionism. And, of course, good interventionism is the professor's own brand only.

6. "Positive" Policies versus "Negative" Policies

In dealing with the ascent of modern statism, socialism, and interventionism, one must not neglect the preponderant role played by the pressure groups and lobbies of civil servants and those university graduates who longed for government jobs. Two associations were paramount in Europe's progress toward "social reform": the Fabian Society in England and the *Verein für Sozialpolitik* in Germany. The Fabian Society had in its earlier days a "wholly disproportionate representation of civil servants."[11] With regard to the *Verein für Sozialpolitik*, one of its founders and most eminent leaders, Professor Lujo Brentano, admitted that at the beginning it called no other response than from the civil servants.[12]

It is not surprising that the civil-service mentality was reflected in the semantic practices of the new factions. Seen from the point of view of the particular group interests of the bureaucrats, every measure that makes the government's payroll swell is progress. Politicians who favor such a measure make a *positive* contribution to welfare, while those who object are *negative*. Very soon this linguistic innovation became general. The interventionists, in claiming for themselves the appellation "liberal," explained that they, of course, were liberals with a positive program as distinguished from the merely negative program of the "orthodox" laissez faire people.

Thus he who advocates tariffs, censorship, foreign exchange control, and price control supports a positive program that will provide jobs for customs officers, censors, and employees of the offices for price control and foreign exchange control. But free traders and advocates of the freedom of the press are bad citizens; they are negative. Laissez faire is the embodiment of negativism, while socialism, in converting all people into government employees, is 100 percent positive. The more a former liberal completes his defection from liberalism and approaches socialism, the more "positive" does he become.

It is hardly necessary to stress that this is all nonsense. Whether an idea is enunciated in an affirmative or in a negative proposition depends entirely on the form which the author chooses to give it. The "negative" proposition, *I am against censorship*, is identical with the "positive" proposition, *I am in favor of everybody's right to publicize his opinions*. Laissez faire is not even formally a negative formula; rather it is the contrary of laissez faire that would sound negative. Essentially, the maxim asks for private ownership of the means of production. This implies, of course, that it rejects socialism. The supporters of laissez faire object to government interference with business not because they "hate" the "state" or because they are committed to a "negative" program. They object to it because it is incompatible with their own positive program, the free market economy.[13]

7. Conclusion

Laissez faire means: let the individual citizen, the much talked-about common man, choose and act and do not force him to yield to a dictator.

Notes

Cf. especially A. Oncken, *Die Maxime laissez faire et laissez passer, ihr Ursprung, ihr Werden*, Bern 1886; G. Schelle, *Vincent de Gournay*, Paris 1897, pp. 214–26

Cf. John Stuart Mill, *Autobiography*, London, 1873, p. 191.

Cf. J. E. Cairnes, "Political Economy and Laissez Faire" (an Introductory Lecture delivered in University College, London, November, 1870; reprinted in *Essays in Political Economy*, London 1873, pp. 232–64).

Ibid., pp. 244–45.

Ibid., p. 250.

Ibid., p. 246.

Cf. W. Sombert, *Deutscher Sozialismus* (Charlottenburg, 1934), p. 213. [American edition: *A New Social Philosophy*, K. F. Geiser, trans. (Princeton, 1937) p. 194.]

Cf. Cairnes, "Political Economy and Laissez Faire," p. 251.

Cf. A. H. Hansen, *"Social Planning for Tomorrow"* in *The United States after the War* (Cornell University Lectures, Ithaca, 1945), pp. 32–33.

Cf. Laski's Broadcast, *Revolution by Consent*, reprinted in *Talks*, vol. 10, no. 10 (October 1945), p. 7

11 Cf. A. Gray, *The Socialist Tradition: Moses to Lenin* (London, 1946), p. 385.

Cf. L. Brentano, *1st das "system Brentano" zusammengebrochen?* (Berlin, 1918), p. 19. The present writer refuted this distinction between "positive" and "constructive" socialism and interventionism on the one hand, and "negative" liberalism of the laissez faire type on the other in his article "Sozialliberalismus," first published in 1926 in *Zeitschrift für die Gesamte Staatswissenschaft*, and reprinted in 1929 in his book *Kritik des Interventionismus*, pp. 55–90.